Hebrews

A Digest of Reformed Comment

D0877647

Hebrews

A Digest of Reformed Comment

GEOFFREY B. WILSON

MINISTER OF BIRKBY BAPTIST CHURCH
HUDDERSFIELD

THE BANNER OF TRUTH TRUST

THE BANNER OF TRUTH TRUST
3 Murrayfield Road, Edinburgh EH12 6EL
P.O. Box 621, Carlisle, Pennsylvania 17013, USA

★

© 1979 Geoffrey Backhouse Wilson
First published 1979
ISBN 0 85151 278 X

★

Printed in Great Britain by
Hazell Watson & Viney Ltd
Aylesbury, Bucks

In thy presence is fulness of joy
Ps. 16.11

CONTENTS

PREFACE

The difficulties which probably account for the relative neglect of Hebrews, as compared with Romans, will not deter those who realize the supreme importance of coming to a right understanding of Christ's Priesthood, and it is hoped that this little book may help to smooth their way through the Epistle.

In this revised edition the text adopted is the American Standard Version (1901), published by Thomas Nelson Inc., and Chapter Summaries have been added. I would again express my thanks to the authors and publishers who have permitted me to quote from their works, and I am especially grateful to Professor F. F. Bruce who encouraged me to make free use of his valuable commentary on this Epistle.

Huddersfield,
January 1978

GEOFFREY B. WILSON

INTRODUCTION

It is certain that the first readers of this Epistle knew its author [13:18, 22ff], but this knowledge has been lost to posterity because he did not put his name to it. Consequently the identity of the writer remains one of the unsolved mysteries of New Testament introduction. Its attribution to the Apostle Paul is more convenient than convincing, and the many modern attempts to establish the author's identity have failed to pierce this veil of anonymity (though Luther's choice of Apollos – cf *Acts* 18:24–28 – still seems the likeliest guess!). However, the providential suppression of the name of its human author is evidently intended to focus attention upon the divine origin of the message itself. When God is acknowledged as the real speaker it is of no consequence if a particular voice he chooses to use cannot be recognized [1:1].

It is almost as great a problem to determine the identity of those addressed by the writer. Some scholars have suggested that it was intended for Gentile readers, but the argument of the letter strongly supports the traditional belief that it was sent to Hebrew Christians. It is reasonable to suppose that they were living in Rome [13:24], where the threat of further persecution tempted them to renounce their faith in Christ and return to the safety of a religion which was acknowledged by the State [cf 10:32–34, 12:4]. The author's treatment of his theme suggests a date shortly before the fall of Jerusalem in AD 70, when the sacrificial system was abruptly terminated by the destruction of the Temple.

Hence this 'word of exhortation' was called forth by the failure of these Jewish believers to grasp the absolute finality of that revelation which God has given to men in Christ. They must understand that those rites and ceremonies under which the gospel was typically set forth in former days have been superseded by the advent of the One in whom they have found their perfect fulfilment. That priesthood in which men 'were not suffered to continue by reason of death' has been abolished by the once-for-all redemptive achievement of Christ who is 'a priest for ever after the order of Melchizedek'. For when the true glory of Christ's heavenly Priesthood is discerned all earthly pretensions to the sacerdotal office must be abandoned.

CHAPTER ONE

The keynote of the whole Epistle is struck in its grand opening statement which introduces Christ both as the revealer and fulfiller of God's last word to men. For though God formerly spoke to the fathers in the prophets, it is only in the person and work of his Son that he has fully revealed himself. Thus Christ, in his teaching office (Prophet), redeeming work (Priest), and heavenly session (King), is the one Mediator through whom we must now make all our approaches to God [vv 1–3]. Since the Jews believed that the law was ministered by angels, it was necessary for the author to prove the Son's superiority over these exalted creatures [v 4]. Hence he appeals to the testimony of Scripture in a series of seven quotations. The first three which are cited set forth the essential dignity of the Son [vv 5, 6,]; the fourth and fifth contrast the obedience of the angels with the sovereignty of the Son [vv 7–9]; the sixth shows that the angels are related to Christ as creatures to their Creator [vv 10–12]; and the seventh points to the Son's present enthronement at God's right hand, whereas the angels pursue their ministries in order to fulfil the Son's commands [vv 13, 14].

V1: **God, having of old time spoken unto the fathers in the prophets by divers portions and in divers manners, 2: hath at the end of these days spoken unto us in** *his* **Son, whom he appointed heir of all things, through**

**whom also he made the worlds; 3: who being the eff-
ulgence of his glory, and the very image of his substance, and upholding all things by the word of his
power, when he had made purification of sins, sat
down on the right hand of the Majesty on high;**

In this sublime announcement of the Epistle's theme its
author is not merely reminding those who had been privi-
leged to receive the divine oracles of the undisputed fact
that God had spoken to the fathers, but he rather seeks to
underline the preparatory and progressive character of that
revelation. In former days God spoke to Israel 'in the prophets'
at various times and in a great variety of ways. These men
were not free to interpret the message they had received
from God in words of their own choosing, for the divine
impulse under which they spoke extended to the very words
they uttered [2 Pet 1:21]. Geerhardus Vos makes the following
comment on the significance of the preposition which is
used here: 'To say that God was speaking in the prophets need
not detract at all from their intelligence, but it does serve
to emphasize the absolute character of the resultant prophecies.
We need not be concerned so much about the *processes* of
revelation, provided we maintain a firm conviction that
the *product* of revelation is truly the infallible Word of God.
This we find in Hebrews, which lays strong stress on the
fact that the revelation was *in* the prophets'.

Among men in general there is unbelief in the Word of God
because it is commonly mistaken for a purely human word
which may be rejected without fear of punishment. Micaiah,
it was held, could not have spoken God's Word, for his
testimony was not acceptable to Ahab, and Jehoiakim at a
later date burnt the scroll which, in his view, was no more
than the pessimistic utterance of a very troublesome prophet.
But God vindicated his Word, and incidentally his servants,
in the judgment which overtook those who opposed it
[1 Kings 22; Jer 36]. Yet that which sinners use as an excuse

for their repudiation of Scripture is in fact the mark of its gracious character. It is for our safety that God veils his glory and sends his Word to us through his servants the prophets who speak as we are able to hear it. For when God did speak directly to the children of Israel they had no doubt that it was God who spoke to them, but they were so terrified by it that 'they said unto Moses, Speak thou with us, and we will hear; but let not God speak with us, lest we die' [*Exod* 20:19]. Those who now stubbornly refuse to hear Moses and the prophets will believe their testimony one day, for there are no agnostics in hell [cf *Luke* 16:19–31]. It is therefore spiritual suicide to neglect that Word which was written by human hands, but which is nevertheless the veritable speech of the living God addressed to our hearts. 'No matter whether written by Moses, the Prophets, or the Apostles of our Lord and Saviour, the one subject of the Bible is the Man Christ Jesus, 'who is over all, God blessed for ever' [*Rom* 9:5]. The testimony of Jesus is the spirit of prophecy, therefore thus saith the Lord himself, 'Search the Scriptures', for Moses wrote of Me, David wrote of Me, the Prophets wrote of Me, and they are they which testify of ME' (Brownlow North, *The Rich Man and Lazarus*, pp. 108–9).

hath at the end of these days spoken unto us in a Son, (ASV margin) It was at the end of these days of Messianic expectation that God spoke his last word 'unto us' in his Son. Christ's fulfilment of Israel's ancestral hope not only brought to an end the period of promise, but also marked the beginning of 'the age to come'. These Hebrew believers could only contemplate a return to the tangible ceremonies of the Levitical system because they had completely failed to grasp the distinctive character of the dispensation in which they were now living. Such a lack of spiritual discernment always leads to the same result, for where ignorance concerning the purpose of Christ's coming prevails, a relapse into some

[15]

form of ritualism becomes inevitable. In former times God spoke to the fathers 'in *the* prophets', but now he has spoken 'unto us in *a* Son'. Or rather 'One who is Son', for the absence of the definite article here underlines the essential deity of him who is *by nature* a Son. 'God spake to us in one who has this character that He is Son' (Westcott). It is the transcendent dignity of the One through whom this final revelation is made which emphasizes the great responsibility of those who are the recipients of it. 'But last of all he sent unto them his son' [*Matt* 21:37]. After sending his own Son, God had no one greater to send. Thus Christ is God's last word to man.

'In opposition to this *gradual revelation* of the mind of God under the Old Testament, the apostle intimates that now by Jesus, the Messiah, the Lord hath at once begun and finished the whole revelation of his will, according to their own hopes and expectation. So, *Jude* 3, the faith was 'once delivered unto the saints;' not in *one day*, not in *one sermon*, or by *one person*, but at *one season*, or under one dispensation, comprising all the time from the entrance of the Lord Christ upon his ministry to the closing of the canon of Scripture; which period was now at hand. This season being once past and finished, no new revelation is to be expected, to the end of the world. Nothing shall be added unto nor altered in the worship of God any more. God will not do it; men that attempt it, do it on the price of their souls' (John Owen).

Since those addressed were faltering in their profession of faith because they entertained an inadequate view of Christ, their instructor immediately corrects this basic error by setting forth his unique glory in seven majestic assertions. The pre-eminence of the Son guarantees the superiority of that revelation which is mediated to mankind solely through him. In these days when the propagandists from the cults aggressively hawk their spurious wares from door to door, it is vital for us to realize that a truncated Christology forms the foundation of all false teaching, and that it never fails to produce a deformed Christianity [2 *John* 7–11].

whom he appointed heir of all things,

1. This was the Father's eternal appointment of the Son to be the mediatorial heir of the universe. For though he possessed a natural authority over all things as the eternal Son, he became incarnate so that through his obedience unto death he might acquire the lordship with which he is even now invested. Moreover, the future universal recognition of Christ's sovereignty over the whole of the created order cannot fail to be realized because it is the subject of this divine decree [*Phil* 2:9–11]. But since grace promises all believers a share in this dominion, John Trapp quaintly exhorts, 'Be married to this heir, and have all!' [*Rom* 8:17]

through whom also he made the worlds;

2. Next, it is explicitly affirmed that the universe was given its existence by the Son's fulfilment of the Father's creative fiat. In his comment on *Col* 1:16, J. B. Lightfoot draws attention to the fact that the Alexandrian Jew, Philo, commonly used the same preposition, 'through' (*dia*), to describe the purely passive and instrumental rôle which he assigned to the Logos (the Word) in the work of creation. However, if the writers of the New Testament adopted Philo's language, both here and in *John* 1:3, they certainly discarded his thought, for in Scripture the Eternal Word is represented as the 'co-operating agent' in the creation of the universe (*Commentary on Colossians*, p. 155). The word which is translated in this verse as 'worlds,' usually means 'ages' (ASV margin), and this suggests the further thought that Christ continues to uphold and direct 'the universe, including all space and ages, and all material and spiritual existences' (A. R. Fausset). None but the Lord of the ages could comfort his followers with the assurance, 'Lo, I am with you always, even unto the consummation of the age' [*Matt* 28:20 ASV margin].

who being the effulgence of his glory,

3. Whereas the previous statements described the splendour of the Son in terms of the Father's decree, in this verse there is a portrayal of what the Son is in his own nature. Here we are told that all the brightness of God shines forth from him who is the very 'radiance of his glory' (Arndt-Gingrich). The divine glory which once rested upon the 'tent of meeting' has been fully manifested in the Incarnate Word who 'tabernacled among us,' 'full of grace and truth' [*John* 1:14 ASV margin]. 'Among the many causes of the extreme attachment of the Jews to the Mosaic economy, this was no doubt one, that such splendid displays of the Divine majesty had been made in connection with it; but the Apostle points them to *the glory that excelleth*, and intimates to them, that humble as was the external appearance of Jesus of Nazareth, He was the true Shekinah, in whom dwelt the Godhead bodily – the real, substantial, adequate representation of the King eternal, immortal, and invisible, whom no eye hath seen, or can see' (John Brown).

and the impress of his substance, (ASV margin)

4. This phrase shows that the Son 'is both personally distinct from, and yet literally equal to, Him of whose essence He is the adequate imprint' (H. P. Liddon). [2 *Cor* 4:4; *Col* 1:15] As Calvin observes, the term 'reminds us that God is known truly and firmly only in Christ. His likeness is not just veiled and concealed, but is an express image which represents God Himself, just as a coin bears the image of the die-stamp from which it is struck'. Although we cannot 'by searching find out God' [*Job* 11:7], yet he is perfectly made known to us through him who said, 'he that hath seen me hath seen the Father' [*John* 14:9]. Thus these two words, 'effulgence' and 'impress', which occur only here in the New Testament, suggest complementary images corresponding to the terms 'co-essential' and 'only-begotten': for it is in Christ that the

revelation of God's glory is seen ('effulgence'), and it is in him that the divine *essence* is made intelligibly distinct for man ('impress'). (so Westcott)

and upholding all things by the word of his power,

5. This impressive declaration attributes to the Son the guiding of all things in the universe to their appointed goal. 'Christ is therefore represented as the *Author of providence* in the broadest sense. To say that He does this *by the word of his power* amounts to an attestation of His *divine* power' (Vos). [*Col* 1:16–17]

'This abundantly discovers the vanity and folly of them who make use of the creation in an opposition unto the Lord Christ and his peculiar interest in this world. His own power is the very ground that they stand upon in their opposition unto him, and all things which they use against him consist in him. They hold their lives absolutely at the pleasure of him whom they oppose; and they act against him without whose continual supportment and influence they could neither live nor act one moment: which is the greatest madness and most contemptible folly imaginable' (John Owen)

when he had made purification of sins,

6. The setting of this statement shows that it is impossible to grasp the meaning of the atonement unless it is seen within the context of eternity. The scandal of the cross is only removed when we understand that Christ suffered 'by the determinate counsel and foreknowledge of God,' and that he did this to make purification of sins. Thus our apprehension of the essential glory of the Mediator will be the measure of our glorying in the cross [cf 2 *Cor* 8:9; *Phil* 2:6–8]. The sacrificial language used here suggests that what was foreshadowed in the purifications prescribed by the Levitical law has been finally fulfilled in Christ's one perfect sacrifice [cf 9:26]. 'By himself' [AV] is omitted by the ASV, but the Greek usage expresses the same thought. As Westcott puts it:

'Christ Himself, in His own Person made the purification: He did not make it as something distinct from Himself, simply provided by His power'. In other words, Christ 'was at once priest and victim – priest to offer the sacrifice, and victim to bear the sin, here considered as a defilement that must be purged away' (George Smeaton).

sat down on the right hand of the Majesty on high;
7. Upon the completion of his atoning work Christ sat down in the place of supreme dignity and power as the enthroned Priest-King of his people [*Ps* 110:1]. In contrast to the Levitical priests who stood during their ministrations because their work was never finished [10:11], our High Priest [8:1] assumed this position of universal authority 'when he had offered one sacrifice for sins for ever' [10:12]. 'Angels and men stand before the throne, the Son sits, not in idleness, but in active power and rule' (R. C. H. Lenski).

*V*4: **having become by so much better than the angels, as he hath inherited a more excellent name than they.**

The author now begins a series of comparisons in order to prove that the superiority of the New Covenant resides in the excellence of the Mediator through whom it is inaugurated. Although this verse refers to Christ's Sonship as the Messiah, his fitness to fulfil this function rests upon that essential dignity which he always possessed as the Son of God [*v* 2]. Christ's eternal ascendancy over the angelic hosts was apparently eclipsed during the baffling interlude of his passion, but his absolute supremacy over them was openly demonstrated when he entered into the Messianic inheritance, and 'sat down on the right hand of the Majesty on high' as the triumphant Son of Man [1:3, 2:7, 9].

Throughout this chapter 'the angels are not compared with Christ merely as exalted creatures, but also as revealers and administrators, in which respects also Christ is superior to them' (Vos). In the giving of the law to Israel God was separated from man by a double mediation – by angelic intermediaries and by Moses – but in hailing Jesus as our 'Emmanuel' we gratefully recognize that in the gospel God himself has stepped alongside us in the glorious person of his only begotten Son [*Deut* 33:2; *Ps* 68:17; *Matt* 1:23; *Acts* 7:53; *Gal* 3:19]. The favourite adjective of the writer appears here for the first time, though it is not difficult 'to see behind the apologetic better the dogmatic best' (A. B. Bruce). [1:4, 6:9, 7:7, 19, 22; 8:6 (twice); 9:23; 10:34; 11:16, 35, 40; 12:24]

*V*5: **For unto which of the angels said he at any time,**
　　　Thou art my Son,
　　　This day have I begotten thee?
　　and again,
　　　I will be to him a Father,
　　　And he shall be to me a Son?

This is the first of seven citations from the Old Testament which are introduced to substantiate the foregoing assertion. Here the interrogative form demands a negative reply, for what is predicated of the Son in *Ps* 2:7 is never attributed to the angels in Scripture. On this John Owen makes the significant observation, 'An argument, then, taken negatively from the authority of the Scripture in matters of faith, or what relates to the worship of God, is valid and effectual, and here consecrated for ever to the use of the church by the apostle.' Thus the silence of Scripture affords no licence for the practice of those rites and ceremonies which owe their origin to the sinful imaginations of men rather than to the positive commandment of God [cf *Is* 8:20]. Angels are collectively referred to as the 'sons of God' in the Old Testament [*Job* 38:7], 'but *Son* is singular to Christ, and incommunicable to any other' (Matthew Poole). 'This day' has no reference to the eternal generation of the Son, an interpretation which Calvin quite rightly dismissed as a 'subtlety', but rather points to the particular time when Christ's claim to divine Sonship was decisively vindicated. Since the resurrection marked the beginning of Christ's exaltation, it makes no material difference whether the fulfilment of this prophecy is referred to that event, as it is in *Acts* 13:33, or whether it is applied to the pre-eminence of the Ascended Christ, as it is in *vv* 4, 5 and in ch 5:5. For as John Murray has well said on *Rom* 1:4, 'Everything antecedent in the incarnate life of our Lord moves toward the resurrection and everything subsequent rests upon it and is conditioned by it' (*The Epistle to the Romans*, p. 12).

The second testimony which could never be ascribed to angels is taken from 2 *Sam* 7:14 and respects the promise which God made to David concerning the establishment of the kingdom under his son Solomon, but it is evident that the primary fulfilment of this oracle did not exhaust its meaning. It also spoke prophetically of the Father's relation to the Messianic Son who 'was born of the seed of David according to the flesh' [*Rom* 1:4], for it was under him alone that the Davidic throne could be established 'for ever' [cf 2 *Sam* 7:13]. As 'the eternal and natural relation that is between the Father and Son' cannot be the subject of a promise, John Owen therefore explains the verse in the following way. 'If it be asked on what account God would thus be a father unto Jesus Christ in this peculiar manner, it must be answered that the radical, fundamental cause of it lay in the relation that was between them from his eternal generation; but he *manifested* himself to be his father, and engaged to deal with him in the love and care of a father, as he had accomplished his work of mediation on the earth and was exalted unto his throne and rule in heaven'.

*V*6: **And when he again bringeth in the firstborn into the world he saith, And let all the angels of God worship him.**

And again, when he bringeth in (AV) The third quotation is apparently taken from *Deut* 32:43 LXX, though the same thought is also found in *Ps* 97:7 LXX. The supporters of the translation favoured by the ASV refer the verse to the second advent, but as the evidence for this is not conclusive it is better to adhere to the AV where 'again' simply signifies the bringing forth of a further proof. It is the constant aim of the writer to make his readers realize that 'the age to come' began with the heavenly investiture of Christ, and it is the present subjection of the inhabited earth to the sovereignty of the exalted Mediator which made necessary a change in worship. Hence the worship which the angels were commanded to pay to Jehovah under the old economy is now transferred to Christ as the 'firstborn' of God's new creation, a term which indicates his 'supreme rank and Lordship' over all things [*Col* 1:15]. It should be particularly noted that it was God the Father who instituted this change in worship, for he does not promise 'to accept any thing but what is of his own appointment; so that it is the greatest folly imaginable to undertake any thing in his worship and service but what his appointment gives warrant for' (John Owen). The verse reveals the foolishness of those who would withdraw their allegiance from the One whom even angels worship, for 'whatever diversity of opinion there may be among men as to worshipping Christ Jesus, there is obviously but one mind and one heart in heaven' (John Brown).

*V*7: **And of the angels he saith,**
Who maketh his angels winds,
And his ministers a flame of fire:

In the fourth quotation, this time from *Ps* 104:4, the word 'maketh' underlines the inferiority of the angels to the Son. 'He is the Son; they are the creatures of God. *Only begotten* is the description of His mode of existence; *made* is the description of theirs. *All* their powers are communicated powers; and however high they may stand in the scale of creation, it is in that scale they stand, which places them infinitely below Him, who is so the Son of God as to be "God over all, blessed for ever"' (John Brown). This graphic description of the angels' service does not imply any transformation of their essence, but rather suggests that 'they are clothed with God's powers to accomplish His will in the realm of nature' (Thomas Hewitt). [12:18ff; cf Exod 19:16,18]

*V*8: **but of the Son he saith,**
> **Thy throne, O God, is for ever and ever;**
> **And the sceptre of uprightness is the sceptre of thy kingdom.**

*V*9: **Thou hast loved righteousness, and hated iniquity;**
> **Therefore God, thy God, hath anointed thee With the oil of gladness above thy fellows.**

The creaturely obedience of the angels is now contrasted with the divine sovereignty of the Son in this fifth quotation, which is from *Ps* 45:6, 7. As H. C. Leupold says, the vocative 'O God' is the simple and obvious translation, and modern critical attempts to evade it appear to be based on the prior assumption that such a confession of the deity of the Messiah is impossible (despite *Is* 9:6). Yet the king who is addressed as 'God' in *v* 8, is at the same time distinguished from God in *v* 9, which speaks of 'God, thy God'. 'This paradox is consistent with the incarnation, but mystifying in any other context. It is an example of Old Testament language bursting its banks, to demand a more than human fulfilment (as did *Ps* 110:1, according to our Lord)' (Derek Kidner).

but of the Son he saith, Thy throne, O God, is for ever and ever; As God's messengers the angels are endowed with marvellous powers, but they remain creatures who are always subject to the Creator's sovereign will. Incomparably exalted above them is the Son to whom alone this throne belongs. Earthly emperors might indeed blasphemously arrogate divine honours to themselves, but because this King is truly hailed by God as 'God' his kingdom must endure for ever. 'His it was by natural inheritance, as God the Son; and as man united to the Godhead, he inheriteth the privileges of that person. This natural dominion over all things remaineth for ever' (Poole). [*Col* 1:16]

And the sceptre of uprightness is the sceptre of thy kingdom.
Unlike the kings of this world whose decisions are often influenced by partiality or prejudice, the Son exercises his royal rule in perfect righteousness [*Is* 11:5]. Our own history shows that those monarchs who insisted upon their divine right to rule were conspicuously lacking in this divine attribute! But Christ's kingdom is an everlasting kingdom, because none but he could bring in everlasting righteousness [*Dan* 9:24].

Thou hast loved righteousness, and hated iniquity;
During the period of his humiliation Christ proved his undeviating attachment to righteousness and his inflexible hatred of iniquity, wherefore 'also God highly exalted him, and gave unto him the name which is above every name' [*Phil* 2:9].

Therefore God, thy God, hath anointed thee with the oil of gladness This is a description of the heavenly coronation which followed the victorious completion of Christ's earthly ministry. It is to this event that Peter alludes when he told the Jews on the day of Pentecost 'that God hath made that same Jesus, whom ye have crucified, both Lord and Christ' [*Acts* 2:36]. The unalloyed joy of this occasion distinguishes it from that unction of the Spirit which Christ received when 'he was a man of sorrows, acquainted with grief, and exposed to innumerable evils and troubles' (John Owen).

above thy fellows. 'The angels cannot be intended; their inferiority to the Son is so insisted on here that they could scarcely be described as His "fellows". It is most likely that the reference is to the "many sons" of ch 2:10, whom the first born Son is not ashamed to call His 'brethren' [ch 2:11]...
Their joy is great, because of their companionship with Him, but His is greater still' (F. F. Bruce).

*V*10: **And,**

    Thou, Lord, in the beginning didst lay the foundation of the earth,

    And the heavens are the works of thy hands:

*V*11: **They shall perish; but thou continuest:**

    And they all shall wax old as doth a garment;

*V*12: **And as a mantle shalt thou roll them up,**

    As a garment, and they shall be changed:

    But thou art the same,

    And thy years shall not fail.

The sixth quotation is again from the Psalms. *Ps* 102:25–27 LXX is cited to show that the angels owe even their very existence to Christ. This work of creation obviously cannot be ascribed to Christ as man, yet it is here properly assigned to him as the eternal Son who became incarnate for our salvation [cf *John* 1:3; *Col* 1:16]. In *v* 12 the Son is further identified as the author of that cataclysmic judgment which finally shall usher in 'new heavens and a new earth, wherein dwelleth righteousness' [2 *Pet* 3:13]. Despite the apparent fixity of the created order the Word of God declares that the cosmos must suffer change, but Christ continues for ever in the glorious unity of his Divine-human person [cf 13:8]. This should teach us that 'such is the frailty of the nature of man, and such the perishing condition of all created things, that none can ever obtain the least stable consolation but what ariseth from an interest in the omnipotency, sovereignty, and eternity of the Lord Christ' (John Owen).

> *Swift to its close ebbs out life's little day;*
> *Earth's joys grow dim, its glories pass away;*
> *Change and decay in all around I see;*
> *O Thou who changest not, abide with me.*
>
> (Henry F. Lyte)

V13 : But of which of the angels hath he said at any time,
Sit thou on my right hand,
Till I make thine enemies the footstool of thy feet ?

The seventh quotation – *Ps* 110:1 – is introduced by a rhetorical question that demands a negative reply. God never addressed any angel in such terms, but the author plainly infers that he did so speak to the Son. This psalm is cited more frequently in the New Testament than any other, and it is also the foundation upon which the whole superstructure of the Epistle is built. It is the repeated application of the fourth verse of the psalm to Christ which gives the letter its distinctive character, for it shows that he exercises this universal dominion as the enthroned Priest-King, thus combining in his own person two offices which were always kept separate in Israel. In verse one, David hails the Messiah as his Lord because only One who was himself divine could be advanced by Jehovah to the place of supreme power. 'As he was God, he was David's Lord, but not his son; as he was man, he was David's son, and so absolutely could not be his Lord; in his person, as he was God and man, he was his Lord and his son, – which is the intention of our Saviour's question, *Matt* 22:45' (John Owen).

Till I make thine enemies the footstool of thy feet ?
The image is taken from conquerors who emphasized their triumph by placing their feet upon the necks of the con-

quered [*Josh* 10:24; *Heb* 10:13]. Although the word 'till' does not indicate a time when Christ shall cease to reign, 1 *Cor* 15:24 does refer to the end of Christ's mediatorial rule. This passage is explained by Charles Hodge, 'When that is done, i.e., when he has subdued all his enemies, then he will no longer reign over the universe as Mediator, but only as God; while his headship over his people is to continue for ever'. As the church is still constantly attacked by the enemies of Christ it is worth recalling Calvin's timely comment on this verse: 'Certainly if we are to believe what our eyes see, then the kingdom of Christ seems to be on the verge of ruin. But this promise that Christ will never be dragged from His throne but that rather He will lay low all His enemies, banishes from us all fear'.

V14: Are they not all ministering spirits, sent forth to do service for the sake of them that shall inherit salvation?

This question, which requires an affirmative response, places the subordination of the angels in strong contrast with the previous declaration of the Son's sovereignty. As their name implies, they are God's messengers 'sent forth to do service for the sake of them that shall inherit salvation'. This refers to the future possession of the heavenly inheritance. Salvation is a present reality of Christian experience, but its full realization awaits the forthcoming consummation. Those who receive salvation as an inheritance clearly have contributed nothing towards it, and this divine patrimony is bestowed upon none but sons [*John* 1:12, 13]. 'The angels serve in reference to that salvation which the Son, thus exalted above them, has procured for man. *They* stand before God as ministers awaiting His commands, but *the Son* sits at God's right hand: *they* minister to God and man, but *the Son* rules; and everything, even against its will, must bow to His dominion' (Franz Delitzsch).

CHAPTER TWO

It is the distinctive style of the author to interlace his exposition with exhortation, and in the first of these he warns of the danger of drifting from God's great salvation in Christ [vv 1–4]. He next explains that Christ's seeming inferiority to the angels during the period of his humiliation was the essential prelude to his exaltation, which fulfilled the prophecy that promised universal sovereignty to man [vv 5–9]. As the intrusion of sin meant that man's destiny could only be achieved through suffering, it was both necessary and fitting that the Son should become like his brethren, for it is through his vicarious endurance of sin's penalty that he has brought many sons to glory [vv 10–13]. Christ's purpose therefore in becoming man was to deprive the devil of the power of death, and to liberate those held captive by its dreadful bondage [vv 14, 15]. Hence the incarnation was the indispensable qualification for Christ's priesthood. For since his gracious design was not to help the angels but the seed of Abraham, he had to be made like his brethren in order to represent them before God and to make propitiation for their sins. Thus, having suffered being tempted, he is able to succour them that are tempted [vv 16–18].

V1: **Therefore we ought to give the more earnest heed to the things that were heard, lest haply we drift away from them.**

Our author here interjects the first of the warnings with which his argument is punctuated. 'Therefore,' as Christ is so infinitely exalted above the angels, both in his person and his station, how urgent was the need for these Hebrews to give diligent attention to the message of salvation they had heard through the preaching of the gospel [cf 4:2; *Rom* 10:17]. This appeal to the glory of Christ lays the axe to the root of the tree of indifference, for a careless hearing of God's Word always stems from a failure to apprehend the unique majesty of the Mediator [*Matt* 17:5]. It was this spiritual lassitude which had exposed them to the very real danger of drifting away from their desired haven. 'Lapse from truth and goodness is more often the result of inattention than of design. Drifting is a mark of death: giving heed, of life. The log drifts with the tide: the ship breasts the adverse waves, because someone is giving earnest heed' (Marvin R. Vincent).

*V*2: **For if the word spoken through angels proved stedfast, and every transgression and disobedience received a just recompense of reward;**

Since there was a strict enforcement of the sanctions denounced against the transgressors of that revelation which was given through the mediation of angels [cf *Acts* 7:53; *Gal* 3:19], then clearly those who neglect the salvation which was first spoken through the Lord will be punished with far greater severity [*v* 3]. This argument expressly contradicts the illogical notion that despisers of the gospel will be treated with greater leniency than those who disobeyed the law of Moses [*Matt* 11:20–24]. For if then 'every transgression' (each stepping aside from the law) and 'disobedience' (which results from an unwillingness to hear) received its *exact requital* or *just penalty*, those who now disregard the gospel must expect a judgment commensurate with the gravity of their guilt in refusing to heed God's own Son.

V3 : **how shall we escape, if we neglect so great a salvation? which having at the first been spoken through the Lord, was confirmed unto us by them that heard;**

how shall we escape, By expressing the warning in the form of a question, the writer appeals to the readers' own judgment, and thus makes his dissuasive from their contemplated apostasy far more effective than if he had positively declared, 'we shall not escape'.

if we neglect To slight the gospel by neglect amounts to a rejection of its proffered pardon, and will be judged as such. 'Can any man perish more justly than they who refuse to be saved?' (John Owen).

so great a salvation? To believe the gospel is actually to receive that salvation, the greatness of which is beyond our computation and comprehension [*John* 3:16]. Thus the proper end in the publishing of the gospel is the salvation of those to whom it is sent; the incidental result is the damnation of those who spurn it [*John* 12:48; *2 Cor* 2:15, 16].

which having at the first been spoken through the Lord, The greatness of this salvation is attested by three indisputable facts [*vv* 3, 4]. 1. It was directly introduced by the Lord himself. As the promised prophet [*Deut* 18:18, 19], he 'came preaching the gospel of God' [*Mark* 1:14], and his own witness to himself gave the apostolic preaching not only its basis and content, but also its authority and power [*Luke* 4:21, 24:44ff].

was confirmed unto us by them that heard; 2. It was faithfully transmitted to us by Christ's appointed witnesses. 'We heard it [*v* 1] from those who heard, the immediate followers of the Lord. The writer thus puts himself in the second generation of Christians. They are not said to have heard the gospel directly from the Lord. Paul, on the other hand, claims that he received the gospel directly from Christ [*Gal* 1:11]' (Vincent).

V4: God also bearing witness with them, both by signs and wonders, and by manifold powers, and by gifts of the Holy Spirit, according to his own will.

God also bearing witness with them, 3. It was evidenced by signs and wonders, manifold deeds of power, and the supernatural endowments of the Spirit. This confident appeal to the miraculous display of divine power which accompanied the apostolic proclamation of the gospel obviously could never have been made if the wonders here described were completely unknown to the recipients of this Epistle. But it is equally unreasonable to expect the continuous manifestation of similar signs when there is now no new gospel to confirm and the canon of Scripture is complete. These gifts 'were part of the credentials of the Apostles as the authoritative agents of God in founding the church. Their function thus confined them to distinctively the Apostolic Church, and they necessarily passed away with it' (B. B. Warfield). So also A. W. Pink: 'As there were *offices* extraordinary (apostles and prophets) at the beginning of our dispensation, so there were *gifts* extraordinary; and as successors were *not* appointed for the former, so a continuance was never intended for the latter. . .We no longer have the apostles with us and therefore the supernatural gifts (the communication of which was an essential part of "the *signs* of an apostle" – 2 *Cor* 12:12) are absent'.

V5: For not unto angels did he subject the world to come, whereof we speak.

These Hebrews had become discouraged partly because they did not as yet possess those external blessings which they associated with the world to come. Their preoccupation with the future had made them blind to their present spiritual privileges, a disease which the author seeks to cure by insisting upon the reality of Christ's present rule. The old world was placed in subjection to the angels when sin broke man's dominion over it, but the new world began with the heavenly enthronement of Christ as the victorious Son of Man. Christianity 'thus marks the beginning of the future world. The author speaks of the great salvation of Christianity, which is so great because God has subjected the inhabited world to the rule of His people. This was the original goal of creation, but it was effected only in Christ. With Christ, therefore, we have a new creation' (Vos).

*V*6: **But one hath somewhere testified saying,**
　　What is man, that thou art mindful of him?
　　or the Son of man, that thou visitest him?
*V*7: **Thou madest him a little lower than the angels;**
　　Thou crownedst him with glory and honour
　　And didst set him over the works of thy hands:
*V*8a: **Thou didst put all things in subjection under his**
　　feet.

In confirmation of his contention the author reminds his readers of a passage of Scripture which is well known to them, even if he has yet to teach them its prophetic meaning – Ps 8:4–6. The Psalmist is filled with awe as he surveys the vastness of the heavens, and he marvels at the Creator's goodness in appointing frail and feeble man to the high dignity of being his vice-regent on earth. With man's *exaltation* over the created order in mind, it was natural for David to say that man was made only 'a little lower than the angels'. But like every prophet he spoke better than he knew at the time [1 *Pet* 1:10, 11], and the inspiration of the same Spirit here leads this 'minister of the new covenant' to apply the same phrase to the *humiliation* of Christ [*v* 9]. For as Westcott says, 'Words which were used of man in himself became first true of One Who being more than man took man's nature upon

Him. In such a case the description of dignity was of necessity converted initially into a description of condescension'. Thus the destiny which Adam forfeited through sin was regained and realized through the obedience of the Son of Man who endured the shame of the cross for the sake of the joy that was set before him [12:2].

*V*8b: **For in that he subjected all things unto him, he left nothing that is not subject to him. But now we see not yet all things subjected to him.**

Although the author's repetition of 'all things' shows that God has excepted nothing from the dominion of man, present experience sadly proves that the full accomplishment of this divine decree is still awaited.

*V*9: **But we behold him who hath been made a little lower than the angels, even Jesus, because of the suffering of death crowned with glory and honour, that by the grace of God he should taste of death for every man.**

However, the application of the prophecy to Jesus exhibits the certainty of its realization, for faith perceives that the final glorification of the members is guaranteed by the present exaltation of the Head. And the fact that Jesus is now 'crowned with glory and honour' is here represented as the abiding consequence of the matchless stoop which had made him 'a little lower than the angels'. 'In becoming man Christ took upon Him a nature that was *capable* of dying. This the angels were not; and in *this* respect He was, for a season, made lower than they' (A. W. Pink). Yet his death was no peaceful quietus, for he willingly came to drain to its bitterest dregs the cup which our sins had mingled (James Denney).

that The word expresses purpose and introduces the clause which explains the reason for Christ's death.

by the grace of God 'This intimates that unmerited grace prompted God to give His Son, and to transfer guilt to Him. In short, whatever was vicarious was of grace in a special sense. A penal death was the effect of justice; but to admit a Surety-substitution was of grace' (George Smeaton).

he should taste of death 'So that Christ by tasting of death had experience, knew what was in death, as threatened unto sinners. He found out and understood what bitterness was in that cup wherein it was given him' (John Owen).

for every man. The scope of this declaration is determined by the context, which shows that Christ died for 'them that shall inherit salvation' [1:14], the 'many sons' [2:10], those who are 'sanctified' [2:11], his 'brethren' [2:11, 12], and the 'children' whom God had given him [2:13]. 'Christ did taste death for every son to be brought to glory and for all the children whom God had given to him. But there is not the slightest warrant in this text to extend the reference of the vicarious death of Christ beyond those who are most expressly referred to in the context. This text shows how plausible off-hand quotation may be and yet how baseless is such an appeal in support of a doctrine of universal atonement' (John Murray, *Redemption Accomplished and Applied*, p. 61).

*V*10: **For it became him, for whom are all things, and through whom are all things, in bringing many sons unto glory, to make the author of their salvation perfect through sufferings.**

Although man idly dreams of salvation without atonement, this is a forcible reminder that it can never be safe to dispense with what is deemed to be necessary by him who is the Creator of all things and the sovereign Disposer of all events. The readers of the Epistle must resist the temptation to renounce their faith in a crucified Messiah, because the glorification of the 'many sons' could only be secured through the humiliation of their redeeming Head, who thus became the 'author' of their salvation. As Geerhardus Vos points out, the word 'perfect' does not mean that 'Christ stood in need of *moral* improvement'. It rather indicates that his endurance of these sufferings perfectly fitted him to exercise this office for his people: 'Christ draws us after Himself to salvation. He led the way to glory' (Vos). [cf *Acts* 3:15] 'Such is the desert of sin, and such is the immutability of the justice of God, that there was no way possible to bring sinners unto glory but by the death and sufferings of the Son of God, who undertook to be the captain of their salvation' (John Owen).

*V*11: **For both he that sanctifieth and they that are sanctified are all of one: for which cause he is not ashamed to call them brethren,**

The character of this salvation is further defined by this description of the work which Christ performs for his people. He is the author of their sanctification. This does not here refer to a continuous process; it means that Christ has cleansed his people from their sin in order to make them fit to serve God. As Vos observes, 'Purifying, sanctifying, perfecting, lie with Paul in the moral subjective sphere, as is especially clear in the case of 'sanctification.' But in Hebrews the last named [i.e. sanctification] has as a rule nothing to do with the subjective moral transformation of the believer. It describes, on the contrary, what has been done through the sacrifice of Jesus outside of the believer, to render the way to God open for him. In Pauline language we should call this "justification," although that would not exactly reproduce the point of view' (*The Self-Disclosure of Jesus*, p. 301).

Now it is because the sanctifier and the sanctified are partakers of the same nature that 'he is not ashamed to call them brethren.' Pink points out that if 'all of one' alluded to God as their common Father this denial of shame would have been entirely out of place, for 'he could not then do otherwise than call them brethren'. But in fact the whole passage is intended to bring out 'the oneness of Christ with His people in their humiliation. In other words, the apostle is not here speaking of our being lifted up to Christ's level, but of His coming down to ours'.

*V*12: **saying,**
> **I will declare thy name unto my brethren,**
> **In the midst of the congregation will I sing thy praise.**

Three testimonies are next introduced to prove that Christ is the Head of a new order of humanity, the first of which is from *Ps* 22:22. This is from that part of the psalm which predicts the triumphant sequel to the Messiah's sufferings. [cf *John* 20:17]. 'The constitution of the *congregation* or 'church' (Gk. *ekklēsia*), with Christ in the midst revealing God to His brethren, is possible only because of His sacrifice' (A. M. Stibbs).

*V*13: **And again, I will put my trust in him. And again, Behold, I and the children whom God hath given me.**

It is because the national rejection of the Messiah was foreshadowed by Isaiah's own experience that his words are here fitly applied to Christ [*Is* 8:17 and 18]. Although his faithfulness to the divine commission had separated him from the nation at large the prophet continued to trust in God. However this isolation was not complete, for his ministry also resulted in the emergence of an elect remnant, even 'the children whom God hath given me' [cf *Is* 6:13]. 'This identification extended not only to his disciples, of whom we read, but also to his children. These children were given him precisely for the express purpose of being identified with him in his trust in God. They were children of prophetic significance. Centuries later this was repeated, on a higher plane, in Christ. Again there was an unparalleled necessity for Christ to put his trust in God, and also there arose a close identification between Christ and the believers' (Vos). This passage, which is unique in describing believers as the children of Christ, strongly emphasizes his humanity. For Christ could not save the children whom God had given him in the eternal covenant of grace without first becoming their Kinsman-Redeemer, and he could not put his trust in God except as he was made man [*John* 17:2].

*V*14: **Since then the children are sharers in flesh and blood he also himself in like manner partook of the same; that through death he might bring to nought him that had the power of death, that is, the devil;**

'Flesh and blood' were foreign to his existence as the eternal Son of God, but Christ willingly 'partook of the same' in order to secure the salvation of his children. In thus stating the purpose of the incarnation, the author also removes its stigma, for as John Owen rightly insists, 'the first and principal end of the Lord Christ's assuming human nature, was not to reign in it, but to suffer and die in it'.

that through death he might bring to nought him that had the power of death, that is, the devil; The vital truth, which is so memorably expressed in this striking paradox, is that Christ's death was indispensably necessary to free his people from death's fearful bondage [*v* 15]. For the children of Christ could only be delivered from the devil's dominion by his dying the death which was properly theirs. It was his vicarious endurance of the penalty of sin which annulled death's condemning power over them and made it but the portal to eternal life [1 *Cor* 15:55–57]. 'Jesus suffered and overcame death; the devil, wielding death in his hand, succumbed' (J. A. Bengel).

*V*15: **and might deliver all them who through fear of death were all their lifetime subject to bondage.**

'The judgment of God always shows itself in consciousness of sin. It is from this fear that Christ has released us, by undergoing our curse, and thus taking away what was fearful in death. Although we must still meet death, let us nevertheless be calm and serene in living and dying, when we have Christ going before us. If anyone cannot set his mind at rest by disregarding death, that man should know that he has not yet gone far enough in the faith of Christ' (Calvin). [cf 9:27] Scripture proclaims freedom from the fear of death through the finished work of Christ, but the best that atheistic philosophy can recommend to modern man is the free acceptance of death as the natural termination of his existence. Those who choose to experience such an authentic 'existence' thereby deprive themselves of that 'life' more abundant which is found only in the living Lord himself [*Rev* 1:18]. As Robert Reymond puts it, 'Existentialism is fatalistic in its view that death can never be overcome and nihilistic in its view that death is the most proper possibility of human existence . . . Existentialism leaves men precisely where it finds them – lost, and without a Saviour' (*Introductory Studies in Contemporary Theology*, pp. 166–167).

*V*16: **For verily not to angels doth he give help, but he giveth help to the seed of Abraham.**

Although it is true that the verb used here does not directly describe Christ's assumption of our humanity, he could not have helped men without first becoming man himself. The idea of 'help' or 'succour' is by a metaphor drawn from the literal meaning 'of laying hold of another to rescue him from peril' (Thayer). It has this sense in 8:9 where God is said to have taken his people by the hand to deliver them from the land of bondage. Thus it is not of angels but of men that the Son of God takes hold. There is justice but no salvation for the angels who lost their first estate. 'Here sovereign

[39]

grace interposeth, – the love of God to mankind, *Tit* 3:4. As to the angels, he "spared them not," 2 *Pet* 2:4. He spared not them, and "spared not his Son" for us, *Rom* 8:32' (John Owen). 'The seed of Abraham' not only properly refers to the immediate readers of this Epistle, but also fitly includes the whole family of faith [cf *Gal* 3:7].

*V*17: **Wherefore it behooved him in all things to be made like unto his brethren, that he might become a merciful and faithful high priest in things pertaining to God, to make propitiation for the sins of the people.**

Here we are given the first *distinct* [cf 1:3] intimation of what is to be the Epistle's leading theme by the word 'high priest', which 'is a shadow cast before from the great section of chapters 5–10' (C. J. Vaughan). As it was God's good pleasure to help men, it was incumbent upon Christ to be conformed to his brethren in 'all things', sin only excepted [cf 4:15]. Hence our Mediator was taken from among men [5:1], in order that 'he might become a *merciful* and *faithful* high priest'. It is preferable with Westcott to relate both adjectives to Christ's work for men, rather than to refer 'faithful' to God. 'Our High-priest is "merciful" in considering the needs of each sinful man, and "faithful" ("one in whom the believer can trust") in applying the means which He administers'.

The expression 'to make propitiation for' appears here with sins as the object, and as it is obviously impossible to propitiate sin, it has been urged with some cogency that the word 'expiation' should be adopted instead (Cf. H. Bushnell's definition: 'We propitiate only a person, and expiate only a fact or act or thing' – cited by L. Morris). But as F. F. Bruce remarks, 'if sins require to be expiated, it is because they are sins committed against someone who ought to be propitiated'. Christ therefore made propitiation *in respect of* the sins of his people, and it is by this satisfaction of divine justice that he gained access to God on their behalf.[1] As the Jews did not expect a suffering Messiah, the cross was the great stumbling block to their faith in him, but this explanation of the purpose of Christ's humiliation is sufficient to demonstrate its necessity.

*V*18: **For in that he himself hath suffered being tempted, he is able to succour them that are tempted.**

Christ's triumph over the temptations which arose out of his sufferings, gave him the perpetual ability to 'succour them that are tempted.' As Westcott well says 'The power of sympathy lies not in the mere capacity for feeling, but in the lessons of experience. And again, sympathy with the sinner in his trial does not depend on the experience of sin but on the experience of the strength of the temptation to sin which only the sinless can know in its full intensity. He who falls yields before the last strain'.

1. John Owen makes the following important points on the word 'propitiate'. 'In the use of this word, then, there is always understood, – (1st) An *offence*, crime, guilt, or debt, to be taken away; (2dly) A *person offended*, to be pacified, atoned, reconciled; (3rdly.) A *person offending*, to be pardoned, accepted; (4thly.) A *sacrifice* or other means of making the atonement. Sometimes one is expressed, sometimes another, but the use of the word hath respect unto them all'.

CHAPTER THREE

Having shown that Christ is superior to the angels who were the spiritual agents in the giving of the law, the author now proceeds to prove that he is superior to Moses, the human agent through whom God gave the law to Israel. If only they will consider Christ, they will see that though Moses was a faithful servant in God's house, a far greater glory belongs to the faithful Son who rules over it. But to remain in that house, they must maintain their faith in Christ to the end [vv 1–6]. This point is enforced in a second warning, which reminds them of the judgment that overtook their forefathers, who were prevented from taking possession of the promised inheritance by their wilful unbelief. So if they would avoid their fate, they must obey the truth by responding to the 'today' of God's grace in the gospel [vv 7–19].

V1: **Wherefore, holy brethren, partakers of a heavenly calling, consider the Apostle and High Priest of our confession, even Jesus;**

In this chapter the author approaches the problem of proving Christ's superiority to Moses with great finesse, as any criticism of their renowned Leader and Lawgiver would only antagonize his readers and prevent all further discussion. In fact this point was conceded in principle when he established the Son's ascendancy over the angels, for even the Jews did not regard Moses as being equal to them. However, it will be seen that in exalting Christ he does not find it necessary to belittle Moses.

Wherefore, Seeing then that we have such a sympathetic High Priest [2:17, 18], we must look to him alone for help in our time of need [4:14–16].

holy brethren, An address which would remind these Hebrews that the faith they professed at once made them members of a holy brotherhood and separated them from their unbelieving kinsmen [2:11].

partakers of a heavenly calling, The earthly rest of Canaan only faintly reflected the reality of the heavenly inheritance which Christ calls his people to share. 'In the word "heavenly" there is struck for the first time, in words at least, an antithesis of great importance in the Epistle, that of this world and heaven, in other words that of the merely material and transient and the ideal and abiding. The things of this world are material, unreal, transient; those of heaven are ideal, true, and eternal' (A. B. Davidson).

consider The word means 'notice in a spiritual sense, fix the eyes of the spirit upon someone' (Arndt-Gingrich). If the author 'could but get the Hebrew Christians to "*consider* the Apostle and High Priest of their profession," his object of keeping them steady in their attachment to Him was gained. It is because men do not know Christ that they do not love Him; it is because they know Him so imperfectly that they love Him so imperfectly. The truth about Him as the Great Prophet and the Great High Priest well deserves consideration – it is "the manifold wisdom of God." It requires it; it cannot be understood by a careless, occasional glance' (John Brown).

the Apostle and High Priest The prophetic and priestly functions of Christ are here closely conjoined by the single definite article. The writer avoids giving the title 'apostle' to the first preachers of the gospel in 2:4 because he chooses to reserve it for the One whom God has sent into the world and through whom God is supremely revealed to man [1:1, 2]. 'As Prophet, Christ is God's representative to His people; as Priest, He is their representative before God. As the Apostle He speaks *to* us from God, as our High Priest He speaks *for* us to God' (Pink).

of our confession, even Jesus; 'Confession' here refers to the faith or religion we profess (cf NEB), and 'our' is emphatic. 'In "*our* religion" it is Jesus who is *apostle and high priest*, not Moses' (James Moffatt). Christianity superseded Judaism because it saw that the Son was greater than his faithful servant [*vv* 5, 6].

*V*2: who was faithful to him that appointed him, as also was Moses in all his house.

The verse disarms prejudice by according Moses the highest praise. In the household of God, Moses resembles Jesus in his faithfulness, for though he was not without personal failings, his ministerial fidelity was beyond question. 'He withheld nothing of what God revealed or commanded, nor did he add any thing thereunto; and herein did his faithfulness consist' (John Owen). [*Num* 12:7] But the faithfulness of Moses could be exercised only during the limited period of his earthly service; whereas Jesus, in faithfulness to God who appointed him, ever lives to exercise the offices of Apostle and High Priest ('*being* faithful'). [*Acts* 2:36]

*V*3: For he hath been counted worthy of more glory than Moses, by so much as he that built the house hath more honour than the house.
*V*4: For every house is builded by some one; but he that built all things is God.

As Christ is the builder of this household, his glory far excels that of Moses who was but a servant in it and a member of it. Christ is worthy of their worship for the supernatural work of salvation which has been entrusted to him by God demands nothing less than divinity for its accomplishment. It is because Christ is the Saviour of the whole people of God who form this house that he is here said to be its builder. As a member of the redeemed community Moses was no more than a part of the house, though he was the revered leader of the Old Testament heirs of Christ's great salvation. And since Christ built the house of salvation in accordance with the plan furnished by the Father's decree, there is no incongruity in the further affirmation that God is the builder of all things.

V5: And Moses indeed was faithful in all his house as a servant, for a testimony of those things which were afterward to be spoken;

Instead of calling Moses a bondservant, the writer uses another word which suggests that his service was freely rendered, and thus underlines the dignity of his position in all 'God's house' (ASV margin). [cf *Num* 12:7] Yet there was no finality in the institutions and testimonies he delivered to Israel, for these all pointed forward to the promised Messiah [*Luke* 24:27; *John* 5:46; *Heb* 10:1]. Moreover, he plainly acknowledged the preparatory character of the revelation which was mediated through him when he predicted the advent of another Prophet whom God would raise up from among them *Deut* 18:15ff]. 'And here the apostle takes his leave of Moses, – he treats not about him any more; and therefore he gives him as it were an honourable burial. He puts this glorious epitaph on his grave, "Moses, a faithful servant of the Lord in his whole house"' (John Owen).

V6: but Christ as a son, over his house; whose house are we, if we hold fast our boldness and the glorying of our hope firm unto the end.

Moses and Christ are both said to be faithful, but similarity falls short of identity, for faithfulness is to be gauged by the sphere in which it is exercised. The faithfulness of Moses was finite and temporal, but that of Christ is infinite and eternal. Moses was *within* the house as a faithful *servant;* Christ faithfully presides *over* the same house as the Messianic *Son.* In Christ there is therefore a radical spiritual continuity between the period of promise and the age of fulfilment [1 *Cor* 10:4; *Heb* 11:26].

whose house are we, if we hold fast our boldness and the glorying of our hope firm unto the end. Their profession of faith in Christ had marked them out as members of this household, but they must be careful to maintain their personal trust in the Christian hope [*Rom* 5:2]. And believers may rest assured that this is no delusory hope, for Christ himself is the substance of it. Those who fail to continue 'firm unto the end' do not overthrow the doctrine of the final perseverance of the saints; they simply prove that they were never really a part of Christ's house. 'The Hebrews were ever in danger of subordinating the future to the present, and of forsaking the invisible (Christ in heaven) for the visible (Judaism on earth), of giving up a profession which involved them in fierce persecution. Hence their need of being reminded that the proof of *their* belonging to the house of Christ was that they remained steadfast to Him to the end of their pilgrimage' (Pink).

*V*7: **Wherefore, even as the Holy Spirit saith,**
Today if ye shall hear his voice,

As the AV correctly indicates, the parenthetical quotation of *Ps* 95:7–11 is introduced to enforce the exhortation 'Wherefore . . . take heed' [*v* 12]. The relevance of this testimony to the crisis of decision which now faced them is strikingly conveyed in the words 'as the Holy Spirit saith'. In describing this psalm as the authoritative utterance of the Holy Spirit the writer not only points to its inspiration, but also emphasizes the peril of regarding Scripture as a dead letter, for its divine Author continues to speak directly to mankind in it [4:12]. 'Today' refers to that period of grace which God grants to men. Those who fall short of the promised inheritance do so by their failure to respond to the last of these daily invitations. Thus their disbelief of the Word of God is an act of disobedience which effectively excludes them from entering into 'his rest' [vv 18, 19]. God's word is always 'Today,' but it is never safe to presume that he will say it again 'Tomorrow!' [2 Cor 6:2] The author is fearful lest his readers should have reached just such a point of no return, for he compares their situation with that which faced their fathers in the wilderness.

*V*8: **Harden not your hearts, as in the provocation,**
      Like as in the day of the trial in the wilderness,

Harden not your hearts, 'It is to the *heart* God's word is addressed, that moral centre of our beings out of which are the issues of life [*Prov* 4:23]. There may be conviction of the conscience, the assent of the intellect, the admiration of the understanding, but unless the heart is moved there is no response' (Pink).

as in the provocation, in the day of temptation in the wilderness: (AV) 'Temptation' and 'provocation' probably allude to separate incidents, though the names 'Massah' (temptation) and 'Meribah' (strife) are linked together in *Exod* 17:7. If the reference is to Rephidim *and* Kadesh, then these examples of Israel's unbelief which occurred at the beginning and the end of their wanderings in the wilderness suggest that the whole of their course was characterized by a progressive hardening of heart [*Exod* 17:1–7; *Num* 20:1–13].

[47]

*V*9: **Where your fathers tried me by proving me,**
   And saw my works forty years.

In the desert they put God to the test to see if he were worthy
of their trust, and these experiments with the divine government were extended over no less than forty years! This
period of time would be of special significance for the descendants of these doubters, if this letter was written shortly
before AD 70, and it was now nearly forty years since Jesus
had accomplished the new 'exodus' [*Luke* 9:31] at Jerusalem.

*V*10: **Wherefore I was displeased with this generation,**
   And said, They do always err in their heart:
   But they did not know my ways;

'Displeased' is far too mild a word, for the Psalmist expressed
God's vehement anger and loathing with that generation. The
word should warn us that there is nothing impersonal in God's
righteous reaction to man's obduracy. This wrath was called
forth by their deliberate rejection of God's gracious leading.
'Always' points to the permanent and prevailing bent of
their character. As this condition was habitual their case
was hopeless. For though they were so highly favoured with
the knowledge of God's will, they went astray in their heart
'and' (AV) preferred to walk in their own ways ('cared not to
take my road' – Moffatt), thus proving their complete
unfitness to enter into the rest of God.

*V*11: **As I sware in my wrath,**
   They shall not enter into my rest.

As 4:8–11 makes clear, the disobedience which excluded them
from the earthly rest of Canaan also debarred them from
sharing in the eternal rest of heaven, 'for God took their
faith or unbelief in this proximate sense as having an eternal
and final effect' (Vos).

'Old Testament examples are New Testament instructions' (John Owen). [1 *Cor* 10:11]

*V*12: **Take heed, brethren, lest haply there shall be in any one of you an evil heart of unbelief, in falling away from the living God:**

All are affectionately addressed as 'brethren', but each is warned of the peril he faced, for none could abandon Christ without also 'falling away from the living God' [2:3]. It is perfectly safe to depart from the dead gods of the heathen, but it is otherwise with him who lives to make his threatened punishments an awful reality [10:31]. The faithless heart is here described as 'evil' because the root of all apostasy is the primal sin of unbelief [*Gen* 3:1]. It might be thought that 'turning back to Judaism would not be apostasy from the living God; that is the opinion of modernists and their Unitarianism. But the writer calls that unbelief' (Lenski). [cf 6:4–6; *John* 5:23, 17:3]

*V*13: **but exhort one another day by day, so long as it is called To-day; lest any one of you be hardened by the deceitfulness of sin:**

They are urged to improve each day of grace by mutual exhortation in order to escape being hardened by the deceitfulness of sin, which in this particular case 'would be the illusion of faithfulness to the past' (Vincent). Sin first gained its power over mankind by assuming an attractive disguise, but its hideous character is revealed by the Word of God which strips it of this fair façade. It is only when the mask is so pierced that sin loses its power to charm [*Gen* 3:13; 2 *Cor* 11:3; *Gal* 6:7].

'All the devices of sin are as fair baits whereby dangerous hooks are covered over to entice silly fish to snap at them, so as they are taken and made a prey to the fisher' (William Gouge).

*V*14: **for we are become partakers of Christ, if we hold fast the beginning of our confidence firm unto the end:**

'We have become partners with Christ' (A. T. Robertson) is a charitable acknowledgment of their profession which must be proved genuine by their patient perseverance to the end. As Kenneth Wuest well says: 'Again as in *v* 6, the question is not one of the *retention* of salvation based upon a *persistence* of faith, but of the *possession* of salvation as evidenced by a *continuation* of faith'. This expression should not be understood in the Pauline sense of mystical union with Christ; it rather points to their participation in Christ's heavenly kingdom [12:28].

*V*15: **while it is said,**
> **To-day if ye shall hear his voice,**
> **Harden not your hearts, as in the provocation.**

It is probably best to regard this repetition of the quotation as beginning a new section (as in NEB), which enforces the lesson to be learned from the example of their forefathers [*vv* 15–19]. The warning note that is sounded in 'while it is said' is well brought out by J. B. Phillips' paraphrase, 'These words are still being said for our ears to hear'.

To-day. . . The urgency of the appeal arises from the fact that there will not always be this opportunity to hear God's voice. For the doors of God's rest are closed to all who fail to heed this warning and refuse to respond to the voice of grace in the blessed day of salvation.

*V*16: **For who, when they heard, did provoke? nay, did not all they that came out of Egypt by Moses?**

The author chooses to set forth the consequences of Israel's unbelief in a series of questions, because this 'favourite device of the diatribe style' (Moffatt) was better fitted to touch the consciences of his readers than a simple statement of the facts [*vv* 16–18].

For who . . . did provoke? 'The writer would say, "My warning against apostasy is not superfluous or irrelevant: *for*, consider; *who* were they that provoked God? They were those who had fairly begun their journey to Canaan, as you have begun your Christian course. *They* provoked God, so may *you*" ' (Vincent).

did not all. . .? 'They were so numerous that they practically constituted the whole generation of the exodus. So far from its being true that a good ending necessarily follows a good beginning, a whole generation of God's chosen people failed to reach the Land of Promise because they provoked God' (Vincent). [cf *Num* 26:63–65]

*V*17: **And with whom was he displeased forty years? was it not with them that sinned, whose bodies fell in the wilderness?**

As the questions of the previous verse identified those who rebelled against God, so this double question graphically drives home the exemplary judgment which overtook them [cf 1 *Cor* 10:5–11]. 'What a long, long line of graves – the saddest in the world! They came out of the bondage of Egypt under faithful Moses [*v* 5], but they fell as corpses in the wilderness!' (Lenski).

*V*18: **And to whom sware he that they should not enter into his rest, but to them that were disobedient?**

As the word implies ('to refuse belief and obedience' – Thayer), they *disobeyed* because they *disbelieved*. 'Unbelief passed into action' (Westcott). That 'disobedient' thus virtually anticipates the 'unbelief' of *v* 19, shows that the author here virtually treats them as convertible terms. And this usage is in harmony with the Christian conviction that unbelief in the gospel is the supreme act of disobedience [cf *John* 16:9].

*V*19: **And we see that they were not able to enter in because of unbelief.**

And so we see . . . (Lenski). This introduces the irrefutable conclusion of the argument. The exclusion of unbelievers from the promised rest of God is not only an undeniable fact, but also a moral necessity. These people *justly* perished in the wilderness, because they divested themselves of all their interest in the promised inheritance through their unbelief. 'And let not others entertain better hopes of their condition hereafter, whilst here they follow their example; for, – No unbeliever shall ever enter into the rest of God' (John Owen).

CHAPTER FOUR

In this chapter the author draws a parallel between the typical rest of Canaan and the real rest that is offered to believers in Christ. He warns his discouraged Hebrew readers not to follow the example of their ancestors who did not believe the good news they had heard, for God has sworn that the unbelieving shall not enter into his rest. It is true that Joshua did lead the next generation into the promised land, but the fact that years later God repeated his offer of rest through David shows that the true rest cannot be identified with the earthly inheritance. Thus there remains a sabbath rest for the people of God. For it is through Christ, whose work far excels that of Joshua, that the believer is able to enter into that rest in which he has ceased from his own works, and this means that the pattern set by God's creation-rest is now fulfilled [vv 1–10]. Therefore we must strive to enter this rest lest anyone should fall through the same disobedience to God's living and powerful Word, which is quick to discern and punish the first stirrings of unbelief in the heart. For all things are revealed to the gaze of the God with whom we have to do [vv 11–13]. So since we have Jesus the Son of God for our High Priest, we must hold fast our confession and come boldly to the throne of grace to receive the succour and strength we need [vv 14–16].

V1: **Let us fear therefore, lest haply, a promise being left of entering into his rest, any one of you should seem to have come short of it.**

Therefore, while the promise of entering his rest remains, let us fear lest any of you be judged to have failed to reach it. [RSV]

As the promised 'rest' of Canaan only typified the eternal inheritance [3:14], the promise of entering into God's rest remained open. But they had reason to fear lest any one of them should *be judged* to have missed it after the evil example of their faithless forbears [3:19]. This translation of *dokeō* (ASV) gives a better sense than 'seem' (ASV), 'for the knowledge of certain judgment is a greater reason to fear than any appearance of failure' (Thomas Hewitt). Such warnings against apostasy are misunderstood when they are thought to teach that true believers may fall away and be lost. For just as accidents are avoided by obeying the road signs which are put up for our safety, so we are preserved from the dangers of our pilgrimage by paying heed to those warnings which are annexed to the promise of salvation. This truth is further illustrated by Paul's experience on the voyage to Rome. He had been divinely assured that *all would be saved* despite the loss of the ship [*Acts* 27:22–25], but that did not prevent him from warning the centurion that *none could be saved* if the sailors were allowed to desert the ship [*Acts* 27:31]. So those ordained to salvation only obtain it by using the appointed means to that end. Therefore all who know the plague of their own hearts will never deem it safe to dispense with what God considers to be necesssary for their spiritual safety [cf 6:9, 10:35; 1 *Cor* 10:12].

*V*2: **For indeed we have had good tidings preached unto us, even as also they: but the word of hearing did not profit them, because it was not united by faith with them that heard.**

The lesson to be learned from the past must not be lost upon the readers, for their fathers in the wilderness also heard the glad tidings of salvation, but 'the word which they heard did not benefit them, because it was not united by faith with the hearers' (Arndt-Gingrich). As in the parable of the Sower, the fault lies not with the message but with the unresponsive hearts of the hearers. To listen to the gospel while remaining destitute of faith is to come short of God's promised rest. The author wants every wavering Hebrew to understand that faith must be mixed with the preached word if it is to profit those who hear it. 'Faith and the promise meeting make a happy mixture, a precious confection' (John Trapp).

*V*3: **For we who have believed do enter into that rest; even as he hath said,**

> **As I sware in my wrath,**
> **They shall not enter into my rest:**

although the works were finished from the foundation of the world.

*V*4: **For he hath said somewhere of the seventh day on this wise,**

> **And God rested on the seventh day from all his works;**

*V*5: **and in this place again,**

> **They shall not enter into my rest.**

For we are entering into the rest, (we) who have come to believe, (Lenski) Unlike the unbelieving who failed to profit from the preached word [*v* 2], *we* are entering into God's rest because we have believed the promise. For it was through our commitment to the gospel that life became a pilgrimage to the heavenly inheritance [11:13–16], which we shall soon enjoy 'if we hold fast the beginning of our confidence firm unto the end' [3:14].

as he hath said . . . For of the faithless Israelites God sware that they should not enter into his rest, although his rest was ready for man since the completion of the work of creation. This further citation of *Ps* 95:11 [cf 3:11] therefore implies that believers may still enter this rest. 'Wherever there is a promise, there a threatening in reference unto the same matter is tacitly understood. And wherever there is a threatening, that is no more than so, be it never so severe, there is a gracious promise included in it; yea, sometimes God gives out an express threatening for no other end but that men may lay hold on the promise tacitly included. The threatening that Nineveh should perish was given out that it might not perish. And John Baptist's preaching that the axe was laid to the root of the trees was a call to repentance, that none might be cut down and cast into the fire' (John Owen).

And God rested on the seventh day . . . This means that God established the pattern upon which man's life was to be built by following the cycle of his creative activity with this day of rest [*Gen* 2:2]. In Hebrew thought the word 'rest' has a positive meaning and 'stands for consummation of a work accomplished and the joy and satisfaction attendant upon this. Such was its prototype in God . . . For mankind, too, a great task awaits to be accomplished, and at its close beckons a rest of joy and satisfaction that shall copy the rest of God. Before all other important things, therefore, the Sabbath is an expression of the eschatological principle on which the life of humanity has been constructed . . . It teaches its lesson through the rhythmical succession of six days of labour and one ensuing day of rest in each successive week. Man is reminded in this way that life is not an aimless existence, that a goal lies beyond' (Geerhardus Vos, *Biblical Theology*, p. 140).

They shall not enter into my rest. It is significant that the divine sentence pronounced on rebellious Israel is again repeated *after* the testimony which confirmed that God's rest had been available to man from the beginning. For it is an emphatic reminder of the solemn truth that this rest will never be attained by the disobedient [cf 3:18].

*V*6: **Seeing therefore it remaineth that some should enter thereinto, and they to whom the good tidings were before preached failed to enter in because of disobedience,**

In summing up the preceding verses [3–5], the author concludes that it is God's desire that men should enter into his rest, and that this gracious design cannot be frustrated by the disobedience of those to whom this good news was first preached. The refusals of unbelief can never nullify the promise of an entrance into God's rest, for others will be bidden to take their place [*Matt* 22:8–10; *Acts* 13:46].

*V*7: **he again defineth a certain day, To-day, saying in David so long a time afterward (even as hath been said before),**
    To-day if ye shall hear his voice,
    Harden not your hearts.

It makes no material difference whether the author regarded the 95th Psalm as a composition of David's (as in the Septuagint) or whether 'saying in David' simply means 'in the book of David.' What matters is that God is still speaking this word of warning and invitation to these faltering Hebrews through the testimony of 'David.' And if they should choose to ignore these repeated admonitions they have no reason to expect that they will fare any better than those who perished in the wilderness for exactly the same fault.

*V*8: **For if Joshua had given them rest, he would not have spoken afterward of another day.**

Moreover, if this rest had been enjoyed by those who eventually possessed Canaan under the leadership of Joshua, then God would not have fixed another day for entering into it 'so long a time afterward' [*v* 7]. For the temporal settlement of the promised land was but a faint shadow of the true rest into which the people of God are conducted by their 'Joshua' who is, as Trapp says, 'Jehovah our Righteousness'. [*Matt* 11:28–30]

*V*9: **There remaineth therefore a sabbath rest for the people of God.**

The word *sabbatismos* occurs only here in the New Testament and it means the 'keeping of a Sabbath.' As those addressed might feel that their faith in Christ had deprived them of a Sabbath rest, the author seeks to allay these fears by showing that Christ's work invested it with a new significance. The Sabbath was a creation ordinance which placed the day of rest at the end of the six days of labour, but when Adam sinned it became impossible for man to attain the rest of God by his own efforts. This now required nothing less than a second creation, and by keeping the Sabbath on the first day of the week, 'the people of God' gladly acknowledge that their entrance into this rest depends entirely upon the redemptive achievement of Christ. 'Believers knew themselves in a measure partakers of the Sabbath-fulfilment. If the one creation required one sequence, then the other required another. It has been strikingly observed, that our Lord died on the eve of that Jewish Sabbath, at the end of one of these typical weeks of labour by which His work and its consummation were prefigured. And Christ entered upon His rest, the rest of His new, eternal life on the first day of the week, so that the Jewish Sabbath comes to lie between, was, as it were, disposed of, buried in His grave' (Vos, *Biblical Theology*, p. 142).

*V*10: **For he that is entered into his rest hath himself also rested from his works, as God did from his.**

In *v* 9 we have the collective 'people of God', but here the author uses the singular because he is stating a principle which holds good in every case. 'When one, who as a believer belongs to God's people, dies, he enters God's rest and, like

God, rests from his works. It is true of all God's people who have already died and will be true of all his people who shall die at some future time' (Lenski).

*V*11: **Let us therefore give diligence to enter into that rest, that no man fall after the same example of disobedience.**

The urgency of this exhortation stems from the very real danger of falling short of God's rest. Once again the allusion is to those whose carcasses 'fell' in the wilderness, and here the verb points to the complete ruin of any one who follows 'the same example of disobedience' [3:17]. For as Trapp remarks, 'God hangs up some malefactors, as it were in gibbets, for a warning to others'. In order to avoid this unhappy fate it is vital that they spare no pains and make very effort to enter into that rest which is offered to them in the gospel.

*V*12: **For the word of God is living and active, and sharper than any two-edged sword, and piercing even to the dividing of soul and spirit, of both joints and marrow, and quick to discern the thoughts and intents of the heart.**

In case anyone might be tempted to treat God's Word as a 'dead' letter which could be ignored with impunity, the admonition is reinforced by the stern reminder that it is 'living, and active', and so is quick to detect and punish the first secret stirrings of unbelief in the heart. The context makes it certain that the phrase 'sharper than any two-edged sword' has no reference to the activity of the divine Word in regeneration, but rather describes its terrible power to execute the sentence which it passes upon rebels who resist its testimony. The qualities attributed to the Word of God show that it is regarded in its *judicial* power (Fausset). As it excluded the disobedient Israelites from the rest which was represented to them by Canaan, so it shall exclude 'Christian' apostates from the heavenly inheritance. On the expression – 'piercing even to the dividing of soul and spirit, of both joints and marrow' – F. F. Bruce remarks: 'It would indeed be precarious to draw any conclusions from these words about our author's psychology, nor is it necessary to understand them in the sense of the Pauline distinction between soul and spirit'.[1]

*V*13: **And there is no creature that is not manifest in his sight: but all things are naked and laid open before the eyes of him with whom we have to do.**

Since 'everything is open and laid bare to the eyes' (Arndt-Gingrich) of the One to whom we must give account, how important it is for us to strive earnestly to enter his rest. The general sense of 'laid open' is clear enough, but there is uncertainty regarding the metaphor from which it is derived. E. K. Simpson associates it with the wrestler's grip on the throat of his opponent, but it is probably preferable to think of the victim's neck being bent back to expose it for the thrust of the knife. Whatever the truth of the matter, we may certainly agree with Simpson when he says that the figure represents 'either the denuded or helpless plight of all created persons or forces when brought face to face with their Creator and Lord' (cited by F. F. Bruce). Hence Calvin wisely concludes, 'Whenever His Word is set before us, we must tremble, because nothing is hid from Him'.

---

1. J. G. Machen regards the threefold division of man's nature into body, soul, and spirit as a serious error because it encourages what he calls 'an "empty-room" view of the presence of God in the redeemed man.' It suggests that only the 'spiritual' part of man requires renovation, whereas Scripture teaches 'that the whole man, corrupt before because of sin, is transformed by the regenerating power of the Spirit of God.' *The Christian View of Man*, pp. 139–144. See also *Collected Writings of John Murray*, Vol. 2, pp. 23–33, and the full discussion in L. Berkhof's *Systematic Theology*, pp. 191–194.

*V*14: **Having then a great high priest, who hath passed through the heavens, Jesus the Son of God, let us hold fast our confession.**

Having then a great high priest, 'Then' does not denote a logical deduction, but simply serves to introduce the Epistle's main theme, which is to show the superiority of Christ's heavenly priesthood over that earthly succession which it has completely superseded [4:14–10:18]. The assertion is at once a word of encouragement and an emphatic reply to the taunts of their unbelieving kinsmen, who would assail the validity and efficacy of this 'new' religion on the ground that it had no high priest to intercede for its misguided adherents. 'The author not only claims that such a High Priest does in fact exist, but by his use of *great* asserts that He is a person of high distinction and power and, therefore, greater than Aaron' (Hewitt).

who hath passed through the heavens, Jesus the Son of God, The appearing of Jesus in glory affords convincing proof that his sacrifice was acceptable to God and assures his people of the prevailing power of his intercession on their behalf. However, this same Jesus is none other than the Son of God for our author does not speak of the conferment of divine honours upon a mere man, but plainly refers to the exaltation of him who is natively and essentially the eternal Son [1:1–3]. As the Aaronic High Priest passed through the veil into the Holiest place, 'so this great High Priest had passed through the heavens and appeared among eternal realities. So that the very absence of the High Priest which depressed them, was itself fitted to strengthen faith. He was absent because dealing with the living God in their behalf' (Marcus Dods).

let us hold fast our confession. It is a characteristic of the author's style to include himself in his exhortations [cf 4:1,

[61]

11, 16; 6:1; 10:22, 23, 24; 12:1 [twice], 28; 13:13, 15]. They must at all costs maintain their subjective confidence in Jesus the Son of God or else they will never participate in the objective benefits of his great salvation [2:1, 6:6].

*V*15: **For we have not a high priest that cannot be touched with the feeling of our infirmities; but one that hath been in all points tempted like as we are, yet without sin.**

The double negative is equal to a strong affirmation. In case the contemplation of the Son's glory should lead them to suppose that he had no capacity for sympathy, they are given the immediate assurance that in Jesus they have a compassionate High Priest who has fully shared their 'infirmities' [cf 5:2]. Bengel turns the ambiguity of this word to good account by saying that in respect of us it includes the idea of sin, but in respect of Christ it is excluded [cf 7:26]. 'The Son of God, had He never become incarnate, might have pitied, but He could not have sympathized with His people. . .The truth is, He not only can be touched, but cannot but be touched. The assertion is not, It is possible that He may sympathize; but, It is impossible that He should not' (John Brown).

without sin. The meaning is not that Jesus triumphed over temptation, though that is of course true, but that there 'was no latent sin in Jesus to be stirred by temptation and no habits of sin to be overcome' (A. T. Robertson). Yet the fact that Jesus *could not sin* [*John* 14:30] in no way diminishes the terrible reality of his conflict with the powers of evil [cf 5:7]. The sinner who capitulates to the first solicitation to evil cannot claim to have felt the full power of temptation. It was otherwise with Jesus who experienced the anguish of temptation to an unimaginable degree, for his immaculate person was subjected to the continuous assaults of the Tempter.

As G. C. Berkouwer puts it, 'Christ's sinlessness does not nullify the temptation but rather demonstrates its superiority in the teeth of temptation' (*The Person of Christ*, p. 263). Thus, having suffered 'being tempted, he is able to succour them that are tempted' [2:18].

*V*16: **Let us therefore draw near with boldness unto the throne of grace, that we may receive mercy, and may find grace to help us in time of need.**

Let us therefore draw near This gospel exhortation reflects the assurance which casts out the spirit of bondage and fear, and enables all believers to draw near to God in worship [cf *Rom* 8:15]. We have here specifically ritual language. Note, for example, 4:16; 7:25; 10:1, 22. This language is used not only of the believers, but also of the officers in the sanctuary, that is, of the priests. Back of this stands the idea that the priest *brings near* his sacrifice, as well as *bringing near* those who follow him. So we are brought near by Jesus as our High Priest and Forerunner' (Vos).

with boldness unto the throne of grace, We are to be thus always drawing near to God with holy boldness, because we know that through the finished work and present mediation of our great High Priest, we are approaching not a throne of judgment but a throne of grace.

that we may receive mercy, and may find grace to help us 'The twofold aim corresponds with the twofold necessity of life. Man needs mercy for past failure, and grace for present and future work. There is also a difference as to the mode of attainment in each case. Mercy is to be "taken" as it is extended to man in his weakness; grace is to be "sought" by man according to his necessity' (Westcott).

in time of need. Or 'for timely help': 'before we are overwhelmed by temptations, when we most need it; such as is suitable to the time, persons, and end designed [Ps 104:27]. A supply of grace is in store for believers against all exigencies; but they are only supplied with it, according as the need arises' (Fausset).

CHAPTER FIVE

The author next shows that the priesthood of Christ is superior to that of Aaron, because the compassion and divine appointment of Christ fulfil the essential requirements of this office. For every high priest is taken from among men, as he could not sympathize with his clients unless he shared their infirmity, and he must also be called by God to undertake this ministry [vv 1–4]. As to his authority, Christ did not glorify himself, but God appointed him to be a priest for ever after the order of Melchizedek [vv 5, 6]. As to his sympathy, Christ's full humanity was attested by his agony in the garden, for it was through his sufferings that he became the author of eternal salvation, being named of God a high priest after the order of Melchizedek [vv 7–10]. Of this Melchizedek the author has many things to say, which he fears his spiritually retarded readers will find difficult to understand. For though by now they ought to be teachers, they still need the milk that belongs to inexperienced babes, rather than the solid food of the discerning adult [vv 11–14].

VI: **For every high priest, being taken from among men, is appointed for men in things pertaining to God, that he may offer both gifts and sacrifices for sins:**

In *vv* 1–4 it is shown that the Jewish High Priest was required to have a compassionate concern for those he represented before God, and that the effectiveness of his ministrations rested upon the reality of a divine call to undertake this office. These requirements were perfectly met in Christ who became the High Priest of his people by divine appointment, and who is qualified to sympathize with them by his unique experience of suffering on their behalf [*vv* 5–10].

For every high priest, being taken from among men, is appointed for men in things pertaining to God, The mediation of Christ depended upon his kinship with those he came to redeem, for in order to manage the religious interests *of* men, every High Priest was to be 'taken *from among* men' [cf 2:9–18].

that he may offer both gifts and sacrifices for sins: John Owen says that 'the proper and principal work of a priest' is the offering of those 'gifts and sacrifices' which sin made necessary, and therefore 'where there is no proper propitiatory sacrifice there is no proper priest'. Hence the Christian ministry is not an order of sacrificing priests! For Christ's priesthood 'leaves no room for any sacrifice or any sacrificial offering for sin in heaven or on earth. What ministers of the Gospel have to offer of propitiation for acceptance is for acceptance not in heaven, but on earth; is offered not to the Holy God, but to rebel hearts of sinful men. It is to be offered not to Him against whom we have sinned, but from Him, and in behalf of Him, to those who have rebelled against Him. And what they have to offer to sinners for acceptance by sinners is the fruit of the completed work of offering for sins. As regards the great matter of expiation and satisfaction, they must bear faithful testimony to the truth, "It is finished"' (Nathaniel Dimmock, *The Sacerdotium of Christ*, p. 80).

*V*2: **who can bear gently with the ignorant and erring, for that he himself also is compassed with infirmity;**

V3: **and by reason thereof is bound, as for the people, so also for himself, to offer for sins.**

These verses indirectly assert the superiority of Christ's priesthood. For the Jewish High Priest had first to offer for his own sins before he acted on behalf of the people, and it was this knowledge of his own infirmity which enabled him to 'bear gently with the ignorant and erring' (as opposed to the presumptuous sinner, cf 10:26 with *Num* 15:30). He was bound to have a fellow-feeling for those he represented because he was himself a sinner, yet this measured mildness cannot be compared with the boundless sympathy which the sinless Son of God feels for those who have wandered from the way [4:15].

V4: **And no man taketh the honour unto himself, but when he is called of God, even as was Aaron.**

The author here pointedly reminds his readers that in contrast to the corruption of the priestly office in contemporary Judaism, Israel's first High Priest exercised a valid ministry because he was commissioned by God for this service; whereas all worship which is offered without a divine command is performed without divine approval and incurs divine judgment [2 *Chron* 26:16–21]. 'As it is the promise of God to govern the Church, so He reserves to Himself alone the right to lay down the order and manner of its administration. On this I base the principle that the papal priesthood is a spurious one, because it was fabricated in a human workshop. God nowhere commands that a sacrifice should now be offered to Him for the forgiveness of sins. He nowhere ordains that priests should be appointed for this purpose. Therefore when the Pope instals his priests to make sacrifices, the apostle says that they are not to be considered lawful unless perchance by some new and special law they exalted themselves above Christ, who Himself did not dare to take this honour on Himself, but waited for the word of the Father' (Calvin).

*V*5: **So Christ also glorified not himself to be made a high priest, but he that spake unto him,**

> **Thou art my Son,**
> **This day have I begotten thee:**

Christ was like Aaron in that he also did not advance himself to the position of High Priest, but was appointed to this office by the Father [*John* 8:54]. When Christ took his rightful place in heaven, God proclaimed him to be his Son, and it is his essential Sonship which qualifies him to exercise such a perpetual priesthood. Yet Christ's triumphant enthronement did not mark the beginning of his priesthood, for this divine testimony was but the public announcement of that eternal decree by which he was ordained the Mediator of his people. And it was in Christ's priestly offering of himself upon the cross that this decree passed into the realm of historical accomplishment [cf 9:13, 14]. This is the second time that *Ps* 2:7 is quoted; see also the comment on 1:5.

*V*6: **as he saith also in another place,**

> **Thou art a priest for ever**
> **After the order of Melchizedek.**

That God declared Christ to be a priest is confirmed by an appeal to *Ps* 110:4, which also indicates that he belongs to a different order of priesthood from that of Aaron. As the promised deliverer is shown to be a prince of David's line in the first verse of the same Psalm [cf 1:13], it is evident that he can lay no claim to the priestly functions which pertained exclusively to the house of Levi. However, Christ's priesthood infinitely transcends the Levitical order for it is patterned upon the unique precedent afforded by Melchizedek, the Priest-King of Salem, and the Messiah therefore permanently unites in his own person the two offices which were always distinct in Israel [*Gen* 14:18].

[68]

*V*7: **Who in the days of his flesh, having offered up prayers and supplications with strong crying and tears unto him that was able to save him from death, and having been heard for his godly fear,**

The author turns next to the experience of suffering which fitted Christ to be a sympathetic High Priest [*vv* 7–9]. While the phrase 'who in the days of his flesh', would seem to refer to the whole period of his humiliation, the rest of the verse appears to point to his agony in Gethsemane. 'These prayers, accompanied with strong crying and tears, to Him who was able to save Him from death, imply the endurance of penal death. Did he fear the mere corporeal suffering which many a martyr has met with fortitude? Sinless nature no doubt shrinks from death, but it was something of a far other quality which gave rise to the agony and amazement which weighed so heavily on the Son of God, – viz., the second death, the full infliction of wrath at the hand of God, for the sins, not of one man, but of the whole company of the elect. The curse of the law under which He spontaneously placed Himself struck the soul as well as the body [*Gal* 3:13]. More was comprehended than bodily pain, as might be argued from the horror and recoil of the Redeemer from the cup which was to be drunk. Besides, corporeal sufferings would not have sufficed for men's redemption, for He redeemed the soul as well as the body [1 *Cor* 6:20]: He assumed both soul and body; and He offered both in our room, as was necessary to expiate guilt incurred in both and by both. . . Hence, while the Lord Jesus continued amid all His agony the object of divine love as the only-begotten of the Father, He endured all the curse, wrath and infliction justly to be awarded to the sin He bore on His own body. . . Though the Surety was in Himself the beloved Son, He was, as the sin-bearer, under the hiding of His Father's face when He poured out these prayers with strong crying and tears' (George Smeaton).

Now it is said that these supplications were answered because of 'his godly fear'. Yet how can this statement be reconciled with the fact that he died? The solution of this difficulty is found in the conditional nature of the prayers which Christ offered. For though he could not but *wish* that the cup might pass from him, he nevertheless submitted himself entirely to the Father's will, and it was this *definite petition* which was fully granted [*Matt* 26:39; *Mark* 14:36; *Luke* 22:42]. 'The ultimate obedience was learned in Gethsemane, after Gethsemane and on the cross the obedience was only carried out' (Lenski).

*V*8: **though he was a Son, yet learned obedience by the things which he suffered;**

Son though he was, (Moffatt). In 12:5f the author teaches that painful discipline is the lot of all true sons of the Father, and that every son, because he is a son, has to suffer. Jesus, however, had to suffer not because *but although* he was 'Son', which shows that he is Son in a unique sense. As the divine Son [cf 1:1f], 'it might have been expected that he would have been exempt from such a discipline' (Moffatt). But as the appointed Mediator of a sinful people, Jesus had to learn that obedience which found its perfection in atoning suffering, 'even the death of the cross'. Here '*learning obedience* signifies *bringing out into the present conscious experience of action* that which was already present in principle. There is a great difference, of course, between the mere principle and even the desire to obey, and the actual carrying out of the desire' (Vos). [10:7]

*V*9: **and having been made perfect, he became unto all them that obey him the author of eternal salvation;**

and having been made perfect, 'As to the term *perfection* (*teleiōsis*), we must adhere strictly to the meaning *fitting for the office*. The experience of learning was a moral experience, to be sure; but the perfection attained was not moral perfection, but a perfect fitness for His office' (Vos).

he became unto all them that obey him Although this qualification clearly limits salvation to the obedient, it does not ascribe that salvation to their obedience. Christ is the author of salvation, but the reality of our interest in it must be attested by an obedient walk [*John* 14:15]. The words would have particular force for those who were beginning to waver in their profession. 'There is, there can be, no salvation through Christ to men living and dying in unbelief, impenitence, and disobedience' (John Brown).

the author of eternal salvation; In 2:10 'the thought was of Christ going before the "many sons" with whom He unites Himself. Here the thought is of that which He alone does for them. In the former passage He is the great Leader who identifies Himself with His people: in this He is the Highpriest who offers Himself as an effectual sacrifice on their behalf' (Westcott).

V10: **named of God a high priest after the order of Melchizedek.**

'Having been made perfect' Christ entered the heavenly sanctuary and was greeted by God as the High Priest of a more excellent order than that of Aaron. The significance of this designation is explained in the seventh chapter of the Epistle. 'God nameth or calleth things as they are, and as he hath made them; and this was done openly, and with the most illustrious solemnity, at his ascension into heaven, when God set him down on his right hand in the presence of all the surrounding angels, who did all submit to him as their Head and King, and acknowledge him as the great royal High Priest of God, as was foretold' (Matthew Poole). [*Ps* 110:1, 4]

*V*11: **Of whom we have many things to say, and hard of interpretation, seeing ye are become dull of hearing.**

The closing word of the previous verse marks a skilful transition from instruction to an extended exhortation [5:11–6:20]. He has much to say to them concerning Melchizedek as a type of Christ, but he fears that the sluggishness of their hearing offers an insuperable impediment to the doctrine he wishes to deliver to them [6:12]. The obscurity does not reside in the teaching, but in that spiritual insensitivity which is the invariable result of coldness of heart. This crushing rebuke is therefore intended to arouse them from their torpor so that his words may not fall upon deaf ears.

*V*12: **For when by reason of the time ye ought to be teachers, ye have need again that some one teach you the rudiments of the first principles of the oracles of God; and are become such as have need of milk, and not of solid food.**

The charge is substantiated by the reminder that their progress in the faith bears no relation to what might have been justly expected of them. They ought now to be teachers, whereas they still needed to be taught the first rudiments of the faith, and to be fed with milk because they were unable to digest solid food [cf 1 *Cor* 3:1ff].

of the oracles of God ' – viz., of the Old Testament. Instead of seeing Christ as the end of the Old Testament, they were relapsing towards Judaism, so as not only not to understand the typical reference to Christ of such an Old Testament personage as Melchizedek, but even more elementary references' (Fausset).

*V*13: **For every one that partaketh of milk is without experience of the word of righteousness; for he is a babe.**
*V*14: **But solid food is for fullgrown men, even those**

who by reason of use have their senses exercised to discern good and evil.

Their spiritual immaturity was evidenced by the fact that they were restricted to a diet of milk, and so they were 'without experience of the word of righteousness'. The context would seem to rule out any reference to justification, and the expression is probably to be understood as a synonym for the Christian faith. Arndt-Gingrich point out that as righteousness 'constitutes the specific virtue of Christians, the word becomes almost equivalent to Christianity'. On the other hand, 'solid food is for fullgrown men' whose experience enables them to discriminate between what is good and what is harmful. The lesson is plain to see: as indolence accounted for their lamentable ignorance of Christian truth, so every faculty must be kept in vigorous exercise to ensure healthy spiritual growth [*Prov* 13:4].

CHAPTER SIX

If these faltering pilgrims are to press on to perfection, they must leave behind the ABC of the gospel, and advance to a more mature understanding of Christ's person and work [vv 1–3]. Since a refusal to advance would expose them to the dreadful danger of apostasy, the author issues a solemn warning against this sin from which no recovery is possible [vv 4–8]. But despite his stern words, he is persuaded of the reality of their faith by their many deeds of love, and he encourages them to go on to inherit the promises [vv 9–12]. For we like Abraham must patiently wait for God to make good his immutable promise, which has been doubly confirmed to us by his oath. Hence our hope has a sure anchorage within the veil, because Jesus has entered heaven on our behalf, having become a High Priest after the order of Melchizedek [vv 13–20].

V1: **Wherefore leaving the doctrine of the first principles of Christ, let us press on unto perfection; not laying again a foundation of repentance from dead works, and of faith toward God,**
V2: **of the teaching of baptisms, and of laying on of hands, and of resurrection of the dead, and of eternal judgment.**

Although the author reproaches his readers for their failure to assimilate the rudiments of the faith [5:12], it is not his purpose to lay again this elementary foundation, for by now they ought to be able to grasp that solid teaching which will enable them to press on to maturity. It is significant that these 'first principles' of the gospel were also features of Jewish faith and practice, because it would be more difficult for people who were already familiar with these doctrines 'to appreciate their new Christian content than for pagans who met them for the first time' (William Neil). The six fundamentals mentioned are arranged in three pairs, and may have formed part of a primitive catechism.

repentance from dead works, and of faith toward God,
The first word of the gospel is the call to repent [*Mark* 1:15], and this involves the radical redirection of the whole life. For no man can be saved without renouncing his sins, recognizing that they are 'dead works' which separated him from the living God and kept him in the sphere of death [cf 9:14]. The sequel to repentance is here simply described as 'faith toward God', because the author is addressing Jews who are convinced of the unity of God, and he wishes to show them that 'faith in God, the God of salvation, is not distinct from, but inclusive of, faith in our Lord Jesus Christ (as in *John* 14:1)' (Delitzsch).

of the teaching of baptisms, and of laying on of hands,
When the readers were brought to faith in Christ they had been taught the vital difference between Christian baptism and all the religious washings it displaced, including ritual cleansings [9:10] and every other kind of baptism for initiates [cf *Acts* 19:1ff]. In the early church baptism was followed by the 'laying on of hands', an act which was associated with the gift of the Holy Spirit, though the case of Cornelius clearly shows that the coming of the Spirit was not dependent upon it [*Acts* 10:44–48]. 'The main point in Acts is that baptism and the reception of the Spirit necessarily belong together' (E. Lohse, *TDNT*, Vol. ix, p. 432).

and of resurrection of the dead, and of eternal judgment.
Except for the Sadducees [*Acts* 23:8], the Jews also believed
these doctrines, but did not connect them 'with Jesus, who is
the Resurrection and the Life and the Judge at the last day.
The foundational doctrine of Christianity gave Jews what
they could not attain in their work-righteousness and empty
Judaism: the sure hope of a blessed resurrection in Jesus
and the certainty that they would be justified in the eternal
judgment' (Lenski). [9:27, 10:37; *Acts* 17:31; *Rom* 10:1–4]

*V*3 : **And this will we do, if God permit.**

if God permit. It is the author's earnest desire to teach his
readers that doctrine which should lead them to spiritual
maturity [*v* 1], but he fears that perhaps their unbelief had so
provoked God that he would not grant them further light
[cf *Luke* 8:18]. For even the sun's meridian splendour brings
no illumination to sightless eyes! Hence this reverent proviso:
'If God permit'; that is, 'If God give me life and ability,
and you capacity and stability; for many fall away, whose
damnation sleepeth not' (Trapp).

*V*4 : **For as touching those who were once enlightened
and tasted of the heavenly gift, and were made partakers
of the Holy Spirit,**
*V*5 : **and tasted the good word of God, and the powers of
the age to come,**
*V*6 : **and then fell away, it is impossible to renew them
again unto repentance; seeing they crucify to themselves
the Son of God afresh, and put him to an open shame.**

This very severe warning is intended to arouse the readers to a
lively sense of the awful danger which faced them, for what
they calmly considered to be a return to the faith of their
fathers is shown as an act of apostasy from which no recovery
is possible. The author hopes to recall them from the brink
of disaster by an alarming description of those who totally

fall away from the profession of the Christian faith [v 9]. This class of persons once appeared to be truly regenerate but their subsequent course sadly proved that they had 'neither part nor lot in this matter' [*Acts* 8:21].

Many have appealed to this passage as proving that it is possible for the truly converted to fall away and be lost. But this presupposes that what is here predicated of such apostates must point to the possession of saving faith, rather than the temporary enjoyment of great spiritual privileges. For though the 'fruits of the atonement enjoyed by some non-elect persons are defined in very lofty terms' [cf 10:29; 2 *Pet* 2:20, 21], it must 'be marked with equal emphasis that these fruits or benefits all fall short of salvation, even though in some cases the terms used to characterize them are such as could properly be used to describe a true state of salvation' (John Murray, *Collected Writings*, Vol. 1, p. 68).

for as touching those who were once enlightened This refers to their acceptance of the doctrine of the gospel, for unless they had first professed its truth they could not have fallen away from it [1 *John* 2:19]. 'The sin against the Holy Ghost, though similar, is not identical with this; for *that* may be committed by those outside the church (as in *Matt* 12:24, 31, 32); *this*, only by those *inside*' (Fausset).

and tasted of the heavenly gift, '*There is a goodness and excellency in this heavenly gift which may be tasted or experienced in some measure by such as never receive them in their life, power, and efficacy.* They may taste, – 1. Of the *word* in its truth, not its power; 2. Of the *worship* of the church in its outward order, not in its inward beauty; 3. Of the *gifts* of the church, not its graces' (Works of John Owen, *On the Nature and Causes of Apostasy*, Vol. VII, p. 25). [Cf *Matt* 7:22, 23; *Mark* 6:20; *Luke* 10:17–20; *John* 6:70; 1 *Cor* 13:1f]

and were made partakers of the Holy Spirit, 'not by an inhabitation of his person in them, but by his operations in them, whereby he is trying how far a natural man may be raised, and not have his nature changed . . . He is proving by his gifts to them how much supernatural good, and workings towards salvation, they are capable of, without the putting forth of the exceeding greatness of his power to make them new creatures' (Poole).

and tasted the good word of God, and the powers of the age to come, The powers of the world to come are projected into the present age through the ministry of the Spirit in the proclamation of the Word of God. The preaching of the good news is therefore a foretaste of the heavenly state. This emphasis upon 'the presence of the future' would have a salutary effect upon the readers, who appear to have been disillusioned because they did not yet possess the external blessings which they associated with the Messianic Kingdom. To cure them of this religious externalism, the author insists that believers are already in vital connection with the heavenly world. For he shows them in *ch* 12:2f that what belongs to the end 'is *present* for the most part, only certain features of it being reserved for the future. The internal, spiritual part is the important part, and this we have *now*' (Vos).

and then fell away, This fall is final and without remedy. The faith of God's elect endures to the end; temporary faith withers and dies [cf *Matt* 13:20–22].

it is impossible to renew them again unto repentance; Here is the first of the four impossible things which are mentioned in this Epistle [cf 6:18, 10:4, 11:6]. It is worth noting that in the impressive word order of the original language, 'impossible' emphatically stands at the head of the sentence [cf *v* 4 in the AV]. The impossibility resides in the apostates themselves, for the complete repudiation of the doctrine which formerly they embraced means that a further preaching of the gospel would be entirely lost upon them [*Matt* 7:6].

seeing they crucify to themselves the Son of God afresh, and put him to an open shame. 'The apostate crucifies Christ on his own account by virtually confirming the judgment of the actual crucifiers, declaring that he too has made trial of Jesus and found Him no true Messiah but a deceiver, and therefore worthy of death. The greatness of the guilt in so doing is aggravated by the fact that apostates thus treat *the Son of God*, cf 10:29' (Marcus Dods). Hence the heinous nature of their sin makes repentance impossible.

*V*7: **For the land which hath drunk the rain that cometh oft upon it, and bringeth forth herbs meet for them for whose sake it is also tilled, receiveth blessing from God:**
*V*8: **but if it beareth thorns and thistles, it is rejected and nigh unto a curse; whose end is to be burned.**

A telling illustration from the realm of nature sets forth the solemn truth that the hearing of the gospel is fraught with eternal consequences for either weal or woe. The land which is blessed by God with frequent showers of rain is expected to bear useful fruits for those by whom it is tended, but that which produces only thorns and thistles is 'rejected' (the word here has personal overtones, cf 2 *Cor* 13:5ff), 'nigh unto a curse' [cf *Gen* 3:17f], and destined to utter destruction.

whose end is to be burned. 'The end of briers and thorns is the fire, they are to be burnt up by it; and this will be the final issue with apostates, to be destroyed by a Christ whom they have rejected, with eternal fire, *ch* 10:27, 12:29; *Matt* 3:12, 25:41; 2 *Thess* 1:7–9' (Poole).

*V*9: **But, beloved, we are persuaded better things of you, and things that accompany salvation, though we thus speak:**

By means of this affectionate address ('beloved' is used only here in the Epistle), the author seeks to assure his readers that his stern admonition was prompted by a sincere concern for their spiritual welfare, and though 'he had spoken it *unto them*, he did not speak it *of them*' (John Owen). For he had every reason to hope that the past evidences they had given of their faith indicated something more than an empty profession [*v* 10]. The assurance is in no sense a retraction of the warning, but is rather intended to dispel any prejudice which might prevent it from having the desired effect upon them. As 'things that belong to salvation' (ASV margin) had been manifested in their lives, so now they are shown 'the one road they must travel without turning back' (G. C. Berkouwer, *Faith and Perseverance*, p. 119).

*V*10: **for God is not unrighteous to forget your work and the love which ye showed toward his name, in that ye ministered unto the saints, and still do minister.**

Since God is not unrighteous he cannot fail to reward the service which a reverence for his name inspired, yet this is an award of grace, and not a merited reward [*Luke* 17:10]. 'The butler may forget Joseph, and Joseph forget his father's house; but forgetfulness befalls not God, to whom all things are present, and before whom there is written a book of remembrance for them that fear the Lord, and think upon his name, *Mal* 3:17' (Trapp). In thus ministering to their fellow-believers in distress they showed their interest in the gospel [cf 10:32–34], for 'those brethren who, being loved in and for God, do evidence to these Hebrews that they are passed from death to life, 1 *John* 3:14' (Poole).

*V*11: **And we desire that each one of you may show the same diligence unto the fulness of hope even to the end:**
*V*12: **that ye be not sluggish, but imitators of them**

CHAPTER 6, VERSES 11–12

who through faith and patience inherit the promises.
The author hopes that a consideration of the end of those who
renounce their profession will prove so salutary that each of
them may be encouraged to display that zeal which leads to the
'full realization' of the Christian hope. He does not wish them
to become '*sluggish*, but imitators of them who through faith
and patience inherit the promises'. The use of the same word
(*nōthros*) in *ch* 5:11 shows that it was their 'dullness' in hearing
which made it necessary to warn them against becoming
'sluggish' in their hope. For a careless hearing of the Word
of God at first diminishes and eventually extinguishes the
hope of salvation. But the promised inheritance can only be
possessed by those who entertain a living hope; hence
they are urged to imitate the patient perseverance of their
forefathers, whose faith is so eloquently commended in the
eleventh chapter of the Epistle.

*V*13: **For when God made promise to Abraham, since
he could swear by none greater, he sware by himself,**
*V*14: **saying, Surely blessing I will bless thee, and
multiplying I will multiply thee.**
*V*15: **And thus, having patiently endured, he obtained
the promise.**

God condescended to confirm with an oath the promise he
made to Abraham, for though this could add nothing to the
trustworthiness of his word, it comforted Abraham to have
it so emphatically endorsed. But as none is greater than God,
the only way in which he could take such an oath was to
swear by himself, a precedent which incidentally attests
the legitimate use of oaths in human relations [*v* 16].

Although Abraham knew that the earlier promise of a
numerous posterity depended for its fulfilment upon the child
of his old age, yet he did not withhold that child from
God, and this unquestioning obedience was rewarded by the

solemn ratification of the promise, the substance of which is reproduced in *v* 14 [cf 11:19; *Gen* 12:2f, 22:16f]. Abraham received a partial fulfilment of the promise in this life, and at death entered more fully into its blessings [*Matt* 8:11; *John* 8:56]. Thus the Hebrews are reminded of the illustrious example of their revered progenitor in order to encourage them in the exercise of that patient endurance which results at last in the possession of the promised salvation.

*V*16: **For men swear by the greater: and in every dispute of theirs the oath is final for confirmation.**

The use to which the oath is put in human affairs serves to illustrate the divine oath [*v* 17f]. For when men swear by the greater name of God this has two results, negative and positive: 1. it ends all contradiction; 2. it establishes that which it attests. 'An oath is a decisive appeal to the highest power to close all controversy. Therefore in condescension God interposed an oath to give to His promise this additional pledge of immutability for our encouragement' (Westcott).

*V*17: **Wherein God, being minded to show more abundantly unto the heirs of the promise the immutability of his counsel, interposed with an oath;**

So God 'interposed with an oath' – he acted as his own Guarantor in pledging the fulfilment of the promise – in order that Abraham's spiritual heirs might be assured of his unchangeable resolve to secure their salvation [1:14; *Rom* 8:17; *Gal* 3:26–29, 4:26–28]. 'His word is sufficient, yet tendering our infirmity he hath bound it with an oath, and set to his seal. His word cannot be made more true, but yet more credible. Now two things make a thing more credible: 1. The quality of the person speaking; 2. The manner of the speech. If God do not simply speak, but solemnly swear, and seal to us remission of sins, and adoption of sons by the broad seal of the sacraments, and by the privy seal of his Spirit, should we not rest assured?' (Trapp).

*V*18: **that by two immutable things, in which it is impossible for God to lie, we may have a strong encouragement, who have fled for refuge to lay hold of the hope set before us:**

The complete veracity of God's word is at once a grand incentive to the Hebrew Christians to persevere in the hope which they had embraced and a tacit rebuke for their tendency to waver in that hope. The bare *promise* of God should be sufficient to command their belief, but when it is reinforced by his *oath*, the complete impropriety of continuing to doubt the One for whom 'it is impossible to lie' is apparent. Hence these 'two immutable' assurances afford the strongest possible encouragement to believers to remain steadfast in their profession.

who have fled for refuge to lay hold of the hope set before us: Whatever may be the precise meaning of this metaphor it is plain that it refers to the protection which the Christian hope provides against an impending catastrophe. A burning conviction of the fearful reality of the final judgment saved the first preachers of the gospel from any sense of embarrassment as they solemnly warned their hearers to 'flee from the wrath to come'. Although there may be an allusion here to the cities of refuge mentioned in *Numbers* 35, the context appears to favour a nautical reference. Thus F. F. Bruce comments: 'We are refugees from the sinking ship of this present world-order, so soon to disappear; our hope is fixed in the eternal order, where the promises of God are made good to His people in perpetuity.'

*V*19: **which we have as an anchor of the soul, a hope both sure and steadfast and entering into that which is within the veil;**

Here the Christian hope is likened to the 'anchor of the soul'. The figure is not to be pressed, but simply means 'that we are moored to an immoveable object' (A. B. Davidson). It is a hope that is fixed in the unseen but real sanctuary of heaven. Therefore the stability of this hope 'is undisturbed by outward influences (*sure*), and it is firm in its inherent character (*steadfast*)' (Westcott).

*V*20: **whither as a forerunner Jesus entered for us, having become a high priest for ever after the order of Melchizedek.**

where as a forerunner there entered in in our behalf Jesus (Lenski). The human name of Jesus, placed emphatically at the end of the sentence, points to the necessity of his sacrificial death [cf 2:9–18]. For it was only because he made our doom his own that he has entered heaven as a forerunner 'for us'. The word 'forerunner' is not used elsewhere in the New Testament. 'It expresses an entirely new idea, lying completely outside of the Levitical system. The Levitical high priest did not enter the sanctuary as a forerunner, but only as the people's representative. He entered a place into which none might follow him; in the people's stead, and not as their pioneer. The peculiarity of the new economy is that Christ as high priest goes nowhere where his people cannot follow him. He introduces man into full fellowship with God' (Vincent).

having become a high priest for ever after the order of Melchizedek. This must not be taken as meaning that Jesus did not 'become' our eternal high priest 'until he entered heaven. That is the same as saying that the Jewish high priest became high priest only the moment he entered behind the veil' (Lenski). The clear teaching of this Epistle is that Jesus entered heaven, there to make intercession for us *in virtue of the once-for-all priestly offering of himself upon the cross* [cf 9:11–

14, 24–28, 10:10–14]. The repetition of the word 'Melchi-zedek' marks an adroit return to the point at which this digression began [5:10], and introduces the instruction which was promised on this theme [5:11, 7:1ff].

CHAPTER SEVEN

The author has already adduced the testimony of Ps 110:4 to show that Christ is a priest after the order of Melchizedek [5:6], and now he appeals to Gen 14:18ff to explain why this priesthood is superior to that of the Levitical order. Firstly, the names of Melchizedek, the Priest-King of Salem, who blessed Abraham after the slaughter of the kings, are suggestive of the righteousness and peace of Christ's priestly reign. Secondly, it is significant that nothing is said of his birth and death, for it means that Melchizedek always appears in the narrative as a ministering priest, and this fittingly illustrates the eternal priesthood of the Son of God [vv 1-3]. Moreover, Abraham confessed the superiority of Melchizedek when he gave him the best of the spoils, so that it could even be said that Levi paid tithes to Melchizedek in the person of his father Abraham [vv 4-10]. Now if perfection could have been attained through the Levitical priesthood, then the Psalmist would not have spoken of the rise of a priesthood pertaining to another tribe, for it is evident that our Lord was not of Levi but of Judah [vv 11-14]. And as the permanence of this priesthood is guaranteed by Christ's endless life and God's immutable oath, it has replaced that imperfect order which required many priests, because they were removed from their office by death [vv 15-24]. Wherefore Christ is able to save all who draw near to God through him, seeing he ever lives to intercede for them [v 25]. For it was fitting that we should have such a spotless High Priest, who had no need to offer daily sacrifices, first for his own sins, and then for the sins of the people: for he made the one perfect sacrifice for sin when he offered up himself. For the law appoints weak men as high priests, but the oath which came after the law, appoints a Son who has been made perfect for ever [vv 26–28].

V1: For this Melchizedek, king of Salem, priest of God Most High, who met Abraham returning from the slaughter of the kings and blessed him,
V2: to whom also Abraham divided a tenth part of all (being first, by interpretation, King of righteousness, and then also King of Salem, which is, King of peace; V3: without father, without mother, without genealogy, having neither beginning of days nor end of life, but made like unto the Son of God), abideth a priest continually.

The author now explains how the high-priesthood of Jesus is typically set forth in the brief appearance of the mysterious figure who blessed Abraham after his victory over the four kings, and to whom he paid tithes [Gen 14:18–20]. As in Paul where the gospel-promise given to Abraham is seen to precede the law, so this original interpretation demonstrates that the law 'has no eternal validity as a way of salvation' by showing that Christ's priesthood was already foreshadowed in the same book of Genesis (so G. Schrenk, *TDNT*, Vol. V, p. 1021).

For this Melchizedek . . . abideth a priest continually. Although the intervening description fills in the details of Abraham's encounter with the Priest-King of Salem, the words 'abideth a priest continually' express the real point of the Melchizedek priesthood. This priesthood resembles that of Christ because the snapshot we are given of Melchizedek in Scripture leaves him in the permanent possession of his office. So as we see him in that picture 'which is a prophetic copy of another, he is a priest continually' (Davidson).

John Owen rightly insists upon the fundamental importance of this surprising disclosure for a true understanding of the person and work of Christ. 'The first personal instituted type of Christ was a priest; this was Melchizedek. – There were before *real* instituted types of his work, as sacrifices; and there were *moral* types of his person, as Adam, Abel, and Noah, which represented him in sundry things; but the first person who was solemnly designed to teach and represent him, by what he was and did, was a priest. And that which God taught herein was, that the foundation of all that the Lord Christ had to do in and for the church was laid in his priestly office, whereby he made atonement and reconciliation for sin. Every thing else that he doth is built on the supposition hereof. And we must begin in the application where God begins in the exhibition. An interest in the effects of the priestly office of Christ is that which in the first place we ought to look after. This being attained, we shall be willing to be taught and ruled by him, and not else'.

*V*1, 2a: In spite of the degenerate polytheism of his neighbours, the sacred narrative describes Melchizedek as a 'priest of God Most High', a designation which distinguishes him as a servant of the only true God. He also ruled over the city of Salem, which is almost certainly to be identified with Jerusalem. Moreover, even the patriarch Abraham freely acknowledged the greatness of this man by whom he was blessed [*v* 7], and to whom he gave 'a tenth out of the chief spoils' [*v* 4].

*V*2b: The author finds a typical significance in the words 'Melchizedek' and 'Salem', for the first means 'King of righteousness' while the second refers to the blessings of 'peace' which flow from his righteous rule. *This is ever the order with God.* The peace which is enjoyed by those who dwell in Salem is based upon the justifying righteousness of their great Priest-King. For as Luther says, 'It is impossible for one to have this peace without faith, that is, the righteousness of God' [cf *Ps* 85:10; *Is* 32:17; *Rom* 5:1, 14:17].

*V*3: In this verse the reasoning proceeds on the premise that even the silence of Scripture is pregnant with meaning. 'Melchizedek was an historical person and not eternal, still as a Scriptural figure he was regarded as eternal, being without recorded father or mother or genealogy, and having no recorded beginning of days nor end of life. In these respects he is like unto the Son of God, that is, stripped of all earthly attachments. As such, then, he is also a type of Christ. Thus *as he appears in Scripture* he may be regarded as enveloped in an atmosphere of eternity' (Vos). This refusal to see anything in Melchizedek save that which is taught in Scripture leads Calvin to conclude that, 'In dealing with everything that has to do with Christ we must scrupulously observe that we do not accept anything that is not from the Word of God'.

Melchizedek's priesthood was unlike the Levitical order in that it was not limited to a prescribed period, nor did it depend for its exercise upon a carefully preserved genealogy; for his office was derived from his personal dignity, and in this he resembled the Son of God. For the immeasurable superiority of Christ's priesthood over the earthly order which it replaced rests upon the divine dignity of his eternal Sonship. Hence John Owen pertinently observes, 'that Christ, abiding a priest for ever, hath no more a vicar, or successor, or substitute in his office, or any deriving a real priesthood from him, than had Melchizedek'.

*V*4: **Now consider how great this man was, unto whom Abraham, the patriarch, gave a tenth out of the chief spoils.**

These Hebrew Christians are now earnestly urged to consider an amazing spectacle: here is the respected founder of their race paying the very best of the booty to a Gentile priest!

'Abraham's doing homage to Melchizedek is a plain proof that, in his sacred character, Melchizedek was superior to any of the religious officers under the legal economy' (John Brown).

V5: **And they indeed of the sons of Levi that receive the priest's office have commandment to take tithes of the people according to the law, that is, of their brethren, though these have come out of the loins of Abraham:**
V6: **but he whose genealogy is not counted from them hath taken tithes of Abraham, and hath blessed him that hath the promises.**
V7: **But without any dispute the less is blessed of the better.**

Even though they were brethren in virtue of their descent from a common ancestor, the people were obliged by the law of God to pay tithes to the sons of Levi because the priesthood belonged to them. As Melchizedek obviously had no place in the Levitical line, Abraham did not present tithes to him as a matter of legal obligation, but in voluntary recognition of his superiority as 'priest of God Most High'. In *v* 6 the author draws attention to Abraham's dignity as the possessor of the divine promises in order to enhance the greatness of the One by whom he was blessed, for it is beyond dispute that 'the less is blessed of the better'. Lenski further notes that 'hath taken tithes' and 'hath blessed' are perfect tenses, which are used to convey 'the lasting significance and effect of these priestly acts'.

V8: **And here men that die receive tithes; but there one, of whom it is witnessed that he liveth.**

This verse points a further contrast between the sons of Levi and Melchizedek, for while the former are dying men even as they receive tithes, the silence of Scripture concerning the latter's death is a positive witness to the fact that he lives.

'The actual historical Melchizedek no doubt died, but the Melchizedek of the sacred narrative does nothing but LIVE – fixed, as it were, in unchangeable existence by the pencil of inspiration, and so made the type of the Eternal Priest, the Son of God' (Delitzsch).

V9: **And, so to say, through Abraham even Levi, who receiveth tithes, hath paid tithes;**
V10: **for he was yet in the loins of his father, when Melchizedek met him.**

In fact, 'to use just the right word' (Arndt-Gingrich), Levi 'hath paid tithes' (perfect tense again) to Melchizedek in the person of the patriarch Abraham, whose acknowledgment of this priest was a representative act which involved all his descendants. Lenski enters a vigorous protest against the suggestion that this forms an apologetic conclusion to what even the author regards as an artificial argument. Such objections have no force when countless acts of ancestors are regarded in the same way today! 'Did Adam's act not put death upon all of us [*Rom* 5:12]? When a king abdicates, does that not count also for his sons and for their sons? When I squander my property, do my heirs still retain it? Why speak of Levi as not personally giving assent to what was done by Abraham before Levi was born? Although he was at that time unborn and gave no personal assent, did Levi not share in Abraham's blessing, both that which was bestowed by God and that which was pronounced by Melchizedek?'

V11: **Now if there was perfection through the Levitical priesthood (for under it hath the people received the law), what further need was there that another priest should arise after the order of Melchizedek, and not be reckoned after the order of Aaron?**

If the Levitical order had achieved the end for which the priestly office had been instituted by God, then clearly the

Psalmist would not have spoken of the rise of a different kind of priest [Ps 110:4]. This failure is heightened by the words in parenthesis, for in stating that the people received the law 'on the basis' of this priesthood, the author certainly implies the inadequacy of its mediation in dealing with the problem of sin. For though Israel rendered an outward obedience to the laws which regulated the service of the earthly sanctuary, yet its priests remained powerless to effect that inward cleansing of the conscience which alone could 'make perfect them that draw nigh' [10:1]. Hence the need of another order of priesthood was proved by the defectiveness of their ministrations.

*V*12 : **For the priesthood being changed, there is made of necessity a change also of the law.**

Since the priesthood was the very basis of the law [*v* 11], a change in the priesthood necessarily involved a change in the law. In fact *Ps* 110 heralded the abolition of the entire legal system with all its ceremonial ordinances. The Jews were mistaken if they believed that the Levitical priesthood was established as a permanent institution by an unalterable law. For the law rested on the priesthood, so when God set aside that priesthood, he also dispensed with the law by which it was regulated. 'These means and these laws served their temporary purpose; and when the time came, they had to be changed for something that would be permanent, complete, eternal' (Lenski).

*V*13 : **For he of whom these things are said belongeth to another tribe, from which no man hath given attendance at the altar.**

This change in the law concerning the priesthood was demanded by the Psalmist's prediction, for the One of whom he spoke was excluded from offering the sacrifices prescribed under that law because he did not belong to the tribe of Levi

[*Ps* 110:1, 4]. 'Seeing Christ himself had no right to minister at the material altar, the re-introduction of such altars is inconsistent with the perpetual continuance of his priesthood' (John Owen).

V14: For it is evident that our Lord hath sprung out of Judah; as to which tribe Moses spake nothing concerning priests.

'For as we very well know, *our* Lord is of the tribe of Judah!' David expressed his personal interest in the Messiah when he addressed him as 'my Lord' [*Ps* 110:1], and Lenski suggests that the author's use of the pronoun 'our' is intended gently to recall his readers to their confession of faith in Christ. Many scriptures plainly foretold that the Messiah was to belong to the tribe of Judah [e.g. *Gen* 49:8–10; *Is* 11:1–5; *Mic* 5:2], while the words 'hath sprung' refer to the historical appearance of this promised 'Branch' [*Jer* 23:5; *Zech* 3:8, 6:12].

The lack of a positive appointment to the priesthood in the law of Moses excluded the men of Judah from exercising this office as effectively as if it had been expressly forbidden to them [*Jer* 7:31; *Col* 2:20–23]. 'That a ceremony is not expressly forbidden by Scripture does not warrant its practice, because the Scriptural rule excludes all religious ceremonies which are not of Divine appointment. Their not being commanded is therefore a sufficient reason for refusing them' (Samuel Palmer, The Nonconformist's Catechism, 1773. Reprinted in *Sermons of the Great Ejection*, p. 212, Q. 34).

V15: And what we say is yet more abundantly evident, if after the likeness of Melchizedek there ariseth another priest,
V16: who hath been made, not after the law of a carnal commandment, but after the power of an endless life:

Although the fact that Jesus sprang from the tribe of Judah makes it clear that the law has been changed [*v* 14], this is 'yet more abundantly evident' from the character of his priesthood, which is first described *negatively* and then *positively*.

not after the law of a carnal commandment, (or lit. *fleshen* commandment) 'The Law of the Aaronic priesthood had reference to descent from a particular tribe, to bodily conditions, to marriage, in a word to "flesh", a word which expresses all that which is mortal and perishable. A priesthood created and exercised under such a fleshen commandment can have no effects outside of the principle which regulates it; it can never extend its influence into the region of spirit and life' (Davidson).

but after the power of an indissoluble life: (ASV margin) It was otherwise with Christ whose 'physical death as Man was no dissolution of His eternal life as God' (A. M. Stibbs). And it is because this perpetual life is the inalienable possession of the Risen Christ that he is able freely to bestow it upon his people [7:25].

*V*17: **for it is witnessed of him,**
   Thou art a priest for ever
   After the order of Melchizedek.

In proof of the perpetuity of Christ's priesthood the author here appeals to the scripture upon whose testimony his teaching has been based [*v* 11f]. As Vaughan observes: 'The typical Melchizedek had this indestructible life only from the studied mysteriousness of the Scripture record of him. Christ the antitype of Melchizedek has it in right of His resurrection to die no more (cf *Rom* 6:9f. *Christ being raised from the dead dieth no more . . . but in that he liveth, he liveth unto God*)'.

*V*18: **For there is a disannulling of a foregoing commandment because of its weakness and unprofitableness**
*V*19: **(for the law made nothing perfect), and a bringing**

[94]

in thereupon of a better hope, through which we draw nigh unto God.

The introduction of a 'better hope,' through which we draw near to God [cf 10:19–22], meant the abrogation of the 'foregoing commandment' which brought nothing to completion. 'For, indeed, that law made nothing perfect. It did not make a perfect priest; it did not make perfect expiation; it did not afford perfect peace of conscience; it did not give real, far less perfect, sanctification. If it had, it would have been permanent' (John Brown).

However, in spite of its preliminary character, the ceremonial law possessed a spiritual value because it foreshadowed the grace which was to be revealed in Christ. The rites which were practised under its provisions derived their efficacy from his forthcoming sacrifice, after which the divine authority for their continuance was withdrawn [cf *Matt* 27:51 with 10:19, 20]. Therefore those who still continued to cling to the shadow actually forfeited the substance it had once represented.

'The "better" hope is that which springs from belief in the indestructible life of Christ and the assurance that that life is still active in the priestly function of intercession. It is the hope that is anchored within the veil fixed in Christ's person and therefore bringing us into God's presence and fellowship' (Marcus Dods).

*V*20: **And inasmuch as it is not without the taking of an oath**
*V*21: **(for they indeed have been made priests without an oath; but he with an oath by him that saith of him,**
> **The Lord sware and will not repent himself,**
> **Thou art a priest for ever);**

Moreover, the selfsame scripture provides a further proof of the superiority of the Melchizedek priesthood by showing that God confirmed it with a solemn oath [*Ps* 110]. The fact that no such oath was made in connection with the Levitical order showed the provisional nature of their service, for the legal dispensation was but a preparation for the advent of the Promised Seed [*Gal* 3:17-27]. Westcott points out that the stress laid on the oath suggests the contrast which Paul draws between 'the promise' and 'the Law' in the Galatian Epistle. 'The Law is an expression of the sovereign power of God who requires specific obedience: the oath implies a purpose of love not to be disturbed by man's unworthiness'.

V22: by so much also hath Jesus become the surety of a better covenant.

The sentence which was broken by the parenthesis of the previous verse is now completed. It is the divine oath which distinguishes Jesus (his name being placed last in the sentence for emphasis) as the surety of a better covenant (*diathēkē*). The importance of this word to the author's argument may be gauged from the fact that this is the first of seventeen times he uses it in this Epistle, whereas it only occurs another sixteen times in the rest of the New Testament. R. V. G. Tasker has noted that 'The Biblical covenants between God and man, though they call for obedience and faith on man's part, are essentially divine dispositions, manifestations of His saving grace. In these covenants, though there are two parties, there is one disposer' (*The Gospel in the Epistle to the Hebrews*, p. 16).[1] But though the Mosaic covenant was good, this is *better*, because the fulfilment of its promises is not suspended upon the obedience and faith of its beneficiaries, for even these were purchased for them by their Surety [*Ps* 110:3; cf 8:6-13]. This word 'surety' (*enguos*) appears only here in the New Testament. It means that Jesus 'is the Personal guarantee of the terms of the new and better covenant,

---

1. For a fuller explanation of the word COVENANT, see the magisterial discussion by John Murray in *The New Bible Dictionary*, pp. 264-268.

secured on the ground of His perfect sacrifice [*v* 27]' (W. E. Vine).

*V*23: **And they indeed have been made priests many in number, because that by death they are hindered from continuing:**
*V*24: **but he, because he abideth for ever, hath his priesthood unchangeable.**

A further and final proof of the inferiority of the Levitical priesthood is now brought forward. It is an incontrovertible fact that there were many Jewish high priests because death always made the appointment of a successor necessary. One by one they were stopped by death. But the priesthood of Christ is never-ending, for *he* ever lives to intercede on behalf of his people [*v* 25].

unchangeable Or 'indefectible'. Our author here affirms that Christ's priesthood 'is in its very nature unsupersedable, that finality inheres in it . . . In the one flawless Mediator we descry priesthood at its summit-level. His unique endowments exhaust the requisites of the office and invest it with ineffaceable validity' (E. K. Simpson in *The Evangelical Quarterly*, July 1946, p. 188).

*V*25: **Wherefore also he is able to save to the uttermost them that draw near unto God through him, seeing he ever liveth to make intercession for them.**

Wherefore also he is able to save to the uttermost It follows from the foregoing that Christ is able perfectly to secure the complete salvation of all those for whom he acts as priest. 'Those who endeavour to come unto God any other way but by Christ, as by saints and angels, may do well to consider whether they have any such office in heaven as by virtue whereof they are able to save them to the uttermost . . . All false religion is but a choice of other things for men to place their trust in, with a neglect of Christ. And all super-stition grows on the same root, in all effects or instances of it, be they great or small' (John Owen). [*John* 14:6]

them that draw near unto God through him, Thus the Hebrews must realize that, 1. They can no longer rely on the mediation of a superseded order of priests; 2. They are *required* to come unto God through that 'new and living way' which has been opened up by Christ [cf 10:19–22 *with* 10:25]. 'Attendance unto the service, the worship of God in the gospel, is required to interest us in the saving care and power of our high priest. – Men deceive themselves, who look to be saved by him, but take no care to come to God in holy worship by him' (John Owen).

seeing he ever liveth to make intercession The unam-biguous teaching of this Epistle is that the ministry of Christ in heaven is one of intercession and *not* sacrifice [cf *v* 27; 9:12, 25, 26; 10:10, 12; 13:12]. 'He is a priest now, not to offer sacrifice but as the permanent personal embodiment of all the efficacy and virtue that accrued from the sacrifice once offered. And it is as such he ever continues to make intercession for his people' (John Murray, *Redemption Accomp-lished and Applied*, p. 28).

H. B. Swete warns us against entertaining a purely carnal conception of this intercession: 'The New Testament does not represent Him as an *orante*, standing ever before the Father, and with outstretched arms, like the figures in the mosaics of the catacombs, and with strong crying and tears pleading our cause in the presence of a reluctant God; but as a throned Priest-King, asking what He will from a Father who always hears and grants His request. Our Lord's life in heaven is His prayer. But in the days of His flesh He prayed as we pray, and one of His prayers of intercession [*John* 17] remains to help the Church to realize in some measure the ends which He sets before Him in His intercessory life' (*The Ascended Christ*, pp. 95–96).

for them. Cf *John* 17:9. 'Christ intercedes for *all* those for whom He has made atonement, and for those *only*. This may be inferred from the limited character of the atonement, and also from such passages as *Rom* 8:34; *Heb* 7:25, 9:24, in every one of which the word "us" refers to believers' (L. Berkhof, *Systematic Theology*, p. 404).

V26: **For such a high priest became us, holy, guileless, undefiled, separated from sinners, and made higher than the heavens;**

We are here bidden to reflect upon the perfection of this new Priesthood which is exactly adapted to our case and need. For '*Unholy sinners* do stand in need of a *holy priest* and a *holy sacrifice*' (John Owen). **Holy** describes what Christ is in himself. As befits 'the Holy One' (i.e. the Messiah, *Acts* 2:27), his character is absolutely holy, and his will is in complete accord with that of the Father [10:7]. **Guileless** sets forth what Christ is in relation to men. His complete lack of evil feeling towards men is positively expressed in that loving service which is the fruit of having triumphed over the full power of temptation [4:14–16]. **Undefiled** underlines the inherent nature of Christ's priesthood. As Moffatt notes, the word suggests a contrast between the *real* purity of Jesus and the *ritual* purity of the Levitical high priest [cf *Lev* 21:10–15]. **Separated from sinners** indicates the abiding result of Christ's victory over sin and death [cf 9:28]. This local separateness 'implies no spiritual barrier: rather it is essential to the exercise of the mediatorial intercession, and even to the universal and impartial accessibility (compare *Eph* 4:10, *that he might fill all things*)' (Vaughan). **Made higher than the heavens** explains the previous phrase by enlarging upon the present heavenly glory of our great High Priest

[4:14]. Calvin shows the necessity for this exaltation by his remark, 'No one can unite us with God except someone who reaches to God'.

*V*27: **who needeth not daily, like those high priests, to offer up sacrifices, first for his own sins, and then for the sins of the people: for this he did once for all, when he offered up himself.**

The supreme eminence of Christ's person therefore explains the superior efficacy of his Priesthood over that of Aaron and his successors: for, 1. their sacrifices were frequent, his was final; 2. they were sinners, he is sinless; 3. they offered animals, he offered himself! Thus the verse introduces the idea of Christ's self-offering which is to be fully expounded in chapters 9 and 10.

for this he did once for all, 'The passages which make mention of Christ's ONE oblation, or of His offering Himself ONCE, are conclusive as to the fact of His being a priest on earth; for that word ONCE cannot be understood of what is done in heaven. It must refer to His death as a historic fact, completed and finished here below. It is against all reason to affirm that the sacrifice was offered once, if it still continues; for the expression ONCE, or ONE OFFERING, plainly contrasts the completed sacrifice with the continuous intercession which evermore proceeds upon it. Nor does the Epistle stop there: the analogy instituted between the fact that it was appointed to all men once to die, and the one atoning death of Christ [9:27], leaves us in no doubt that we must view that sacrifice as completed on the cross' (George Smeaton).

*V*28: **For the law appointeth men high priests, having infirmity; but the word of the oath, which was after the law, appointeth a Son, perfected for evermore.**

The disparity is even more starkly displayed in the concluding contrast which crowns the whole argument. The law appointed men with sinful infirmities, but the word of the oath appointed a Son who has been 'perfected for evermore.' This means that 'all sacrifices had been consummated in the one Sacrifice, all priesthoods absorbed in the one Priest. The offering had been made once for all: and, as there were no more victims, there could be no more priests' (J. B. Lightfoot, 'The Christian Ministry,' appended to *The Epistle to the Philippians*, p. 265). Therefore, 'Plurality of priests under the gospel overthrows the whole argument of the apostle in this place; and if we have yet priests that have infirmities, they are made by the law, and not by the gospel' (John Owen).

CHAPTER EIGHT

Since our High Priest is now enthroned in the true tabernacle of heaven, he clearly has a superior priesthood to those whose ministrations are of necessity confined to the earthly copy of these heavenly realities. He is thus the Mediator of a better covenant, which is founded upon better promises, than that which was given through Moses [vv 1–6]. For if the first covenant had been faultless, there would have been no point in the prophetic promise of a new covenant, whose very announcement by Jeremiah implied that the existing covenant was already old and obsolete [vv 7–13].

V1: Now in the things which we are saying the chief point is this: We have such a high priest, who sat down on the right hand of the throne of the Majesty in the heavens,
V2: a minister of the sanctuary, and of the true tabernacle, which the Lord pitched, not man.

In this section of the Epistle the author enters upon an extended comparison of Christ's priestly ministry with that which was exercised by mortal men [8:1–10:18]. The discussion naturally rests upon what has gone before, but the main point to remember is that Christ ministers in the heavenly sanctuary and not in an earthly tabernacle made with hands [9:24]. For unlike those priests who performed their service in the tabernacle erected by man (Moses), Christ is a minister of the *true* tabernacle which was pitched by God himself. This 'does not imply that the tabernacle in the wilderness was not also most truly pitched at God's bidding, and according to the pattern which He had shown [*Exod* 25:40]; but only that it, and all things in it, were weak earthly copies of heavenly realities' (R. C. Trench, *Synonyms of the New Testament*, pp. 26–27).

The greatness of Christ's priesthood is further revealed by the place which he occupies in the real sanctuary above [1:3]. For whereas the Levitical high priest entered the earthly 'holy place' but once a year, and then only to *stand* briefly before the symbol of God's throne, Christ our Priest-King *sat down* on the throne of the divine Majesty in heaven itself! And the essential point which the unsettled readers must grasp is that their unseen Mediator so reigns in glory in order to minister all the riches of his grace to them [11:1].

John Owen makes a characteristically vigorous application of this truth: 'The church hath lost nothing by the removal of the old tabernacle and temple, all being supplied by this sanctuary, true tabernacle, and minister thereof. – The glory and worship of the temple was that which the Jews would by no means part withal. . .And in later ages men ceased not, until they had brought into Christianity itself a worship vying for external order, ceremony, pomp, and painting, with whatever was in the tabernacle or temple of old; coming short of it principally in this, that *that* was of God's institution for a time, *this* of the invention of weak, superstitious, and foolish men. Thus is it in the church of Rome. And a hard thing it is to raise the minds of men unto a satisfaction in things merely spiritual and heavenly . . . But "unto them that believe Christ is precious." And this "true tabernacle," with his ministration, is more unto them than all the old pompous ceremonies and services of divine institution, much more the superstitious observances of human invention'.

*V*3: **For every high priest is appointed to offer both**

gifts and sacrifices: wherefore it is necessary that this high priest also have somewhat to offer.

A priest without a sacrifice is like a childless mother, for he is expressly appointed in order to make such offerings. Therefore if Christ is a priest he too must 'have had something to offer' (NEB margin). The tense of the verb used here definitely excludes all thought of a continuous offering, and as F. F. Bruce observes, 'is consistent with our author's repeated emphasis on the singularity of the sacrifice which Christ offered [cf 7:27, 10:12]'. But 'because Christ's crowning act of priesthood, His offering of Himself, was done in relation to the actual presence of God, and not in relation to the earthly figure sanctuary in Jerusalem, it was, as the writer to the Hebrews saw it, done in the true heavenly tabernacle and not in the shadowy earthly one. In other words, though Jesus died outside the city of Jerusalem, His deed as a priestly act was done in heaven, or in the heavenlies, as Paul himself might have said, and not just on earth' (A. M. Stibbs, *The Finished Work of Christ*, p. 25). 'If any one else can offer the body of Christ, he also is the minister of the true tabernacle. – For the Lord Christ did no more, He did but offer himself; and they that can offer him, do put themselves in his place' (John Owen).

*V*4: **Now if he were on earth, he would not be a priest at all, seeing there are those who offer the gifts according to the law;**

Indeed the mere fact that Christ did not belong to the tribe of Levi prevented him from presenting the offerings prescribed by the law. His descent from Judah meant that he could never officiate as a priest in the earthly sanctuary [7:13, 14], though of course he acted as a priest on earth when he 'suffered without [outside] the gate' in order to sanctify the people [13:12].

*V*5: **who serve that which is a copy and shadow of the heavenly things, even as Moses is warned of God when he is about to make the tabernacle: for, See, saith he, that thou make all things according to the pattern that was showed thee in the mount.**

These priests ministered in the tabernacle which was but a copy of the reality it represented. It provided only 'a pale reflexion' (Souter) of the heavenly things. Nevertheless it was a copy which God had commanded Moses to make, and it was this alone which invested it with spiritual meaning. But this meaning could not be conveyed to men if Moses were permitted to introduce any innovation into the worship of God, and therefore he was strictly admonished to make everything precisely according to the pattern which had been shown to him on the mount.

Hence Calvin concludes, 'By thus emphasizing the rule that He has laid down, He forbids us to depart from it in the very slightest. For this reason all the forms of worship produced by men fail, and also those things which are called sacraments and yet have not come from God. . .We must beware that in wishing to fit our own inventions to Christ we do not so change Him (as the papists do) that He becomes unlike Himself. It is not permissible for us to invent anything we like, but it belongs to God alone to show us *according to the pattern that was showed thee*'.

*V*6: **But now hath he obtained a ministry the more excellent, by so much as he is also the mediator of a better covenant, which hath been enacted upon better promises.**

But as the case now stands, Christ has obtained a more excellent ministry for he is the mediator of a better covenant 'which has been (legally) enacted on the basis of better promises' (Arndt-Gingrich). With this emphatic repetition of the word 'better' the keynote of the Epistle is again struck.

'At every point Christianity is better than Judaism' (A. T. Robertson). The superiority of this covenant lies in the fact that its promises are guaranteed by the perfect satisfaction which has been rendered to God by its Mediator on behalf of those he represented [7:22, 27]. A covenant requires a mediator or 'middleman' to bring together the contracting parties, and Christ effected this union between God and his people by means of that reconciling work which secured the interests of both parties, because it met the claims of justice and mercy. In the verses that follow the author shows that the Scripture speaks of the 'better promises' on which this covenant rests: they consist in, 1. the renewal of the heart [v 10]; 2. the universal knowledge of God [v 11]; 3. the complete forgiveness of sins [v 12].

V7: For if that first covenant had been faultless, then would no place have been sought for a second.

If the Sinaitic covenant had not manifestly failed to produce the obedience it demanded, there would have been no occasion to search for a new covenant to replace it. That such a search for something better was going on even while that dispensation remained in full force is proved by the testimony of Jeremiah [vv 8–12]. The author thus shows that 'the Levitical system answered to a covenant which was recognized as imperfect and transitory by an Old Testament prophet, since he spoke of a divine purpose to establish a new covenant' (Vincent).

V8a: For finding fault with them, he saith,

This appeal to Scripture substantiates the bold assertion of the previous verse [*Jer* 31:31–34]. 'There is a subtle delicacy of language in this insensible shifting of the blame from the covenant to the people. The covenant itself could hardly be said to be faultless, seeing that it failed to bind Israel to their God; but the true cause of failure lay in the character of the people, not in the law, which was holy, righteous, and good'

(F. Rendall, *The Epistle to the Hebrews*, p. 65). 'The old covenant was faulty because it did not provide for enabling the people to live up to the terms or conditions of it. *It* was faulty inasmuch as it did not sufficiently provide against *their* faultiness' (Marcus Dods).

he saith, (*legei*) The significance of this 'subjectless' phrase is well brought out in a comment by B. B. Warfield: 'Like Philo, the author of the Epistle to the Hebrews looks upon Scripture as an oracular book, and all that it says, God says to him: and accordingly, like Philo, he adduces its words with a simple "it says," with the full implication that this "it says" is a "God says" also' (*The Inspiration and Authority of the Bible*, p. 346).

*V*8b: Behold, the days come, saith the Lord,
    That I will make a new covenant with the house
        of Israel and with the house of Judah;
*V*9: Not according to the covenant that I made with
        their fathers
    In the day that I took them by the hand to lead
        them forth out of the land of Egypt;
    For they continued not in my covenant,
    And I regarded them not, saith the Lord.
*V*10: For this is the covenant that I will make
        with the house of Israel
    After those days, saith the Lord;
    I will put my laws into their mind,
    And on their heart also will I write them:
    And I will be to them a God,
    And they shall be to me a people:
*V*11: And they shall not teach every man his fellow-
        citizen,
    And every man his brother, saying, Know the
        Lord:
    For all shall know me,

From the least to the greatest of them.
*V*12: **For I will be merciful to their iniquities,**
   And their sins will I remember no more.

In this important prophecy the covenant which God made
with Israel at Sinai is unfavourably compared with the new
covenant which would eventually supersede it. The author
has no other purpose in quoting it than to prove that its
promises have been fulfilled by Christ and that his church
now constitutes the New Israel of God.[1] As the terms of
the Mosaic covenant were rendered null and void by the
disobedience of the people, God therefore speaks of a new
covenant which cannot be broken because it will ensure
the spiritual response of those with whom it is made by
providing for the internal renovation of their character.
Under the gracious provisions of this covenant, God promises
to inscribe his law upon the hearts of his people, who shall
all know him 'from the least to the greatest', *for* 'their sins
will I remember no more'.

1. **I will put my laws into their mind, and on their heart
also will I write them** [*v* 10] At Sinai the proclamation of the
law was accompanied by the most terrible portents, yet
even this awesome disclosure did not succeed in securing
Israel's obedience to its demands [12:18–21]. Indeed the per-
verse obduracy of the human heart is such that until God
is pleased to renew it by his Spirit it cannot render any
obedience to his law [*Ezek* 36:26–27]. 'It is clear from this
how much force free will has, and what rightness there is in
our nature before God renews us. We will and we choose,
and we do so of our own accord, but our will is carried away
by an almost raging impulse to resist God and cannot in any
way submit to His justice. So it comes about that the Law

1. O. T. Allis subjects the teaching of those who claim 'that the
Christian Church is a mystery parenthesis which interrupts the fulfilment to Israel of the Kingdom prophecies of the Old Testament' to a
devastating examination in his book *Prophecy and the Church*.

is fatal and deadly for us as long as it remains written on tablets of stone, as Paul says in 2 *Cor* 3:3. In short, we accept God's command obediently when He changes and corrects the native wickedness of our hearts by His Spirit; otherwise He will find nothing in us but evil passions and a heart wholly given to wickedness. It is clearly laid down that a new covenant is to be made by which God will write His laws on our hearts, because otherwise it will be of no effect' (Calvin).

2. **all shall know me** [*v* 11] It is clear from the preceding promise that far more is signified by this than mere notional knowledge *about* God. It rather speaks of that personal knowledge *of* God which is ever expressed in a practical conformity to the divine will. This knowledge is neither sacramentally conveyed through a hierarchy of self-styled priests, nor is it individually communicated in any mystical fashion apart from the Word of God. 'No new prophets appear with new messages. We have all God's Word; and each has it in his own hand. We can by it even test those who stand up to preach and to teach it. "From their small up to their great" is correct: from our children and our catechumens up to our great theologians; God's saving revelation, complete at last, is accessible to all alike. It is the fulfilment of the prophecy of Jeremiah and of *Is* 54:13; 11:9; *Hab* 2:14; *Joel* 2:28; cf *John* 6:45; 1 *John* 2:20, 27' (Lenski).

3. **their sins will I remember no more** [*v* 12] The word 'for' which introduces the final promise indicates that the former blessings are based upon a full satisfaction for sin. As the old covenant was not ratified without the sprinkling of the blood of sacrifice, so the new covenant could not be inaugurated without the shedding of Christ's blood [9:19–22; *Exod* 24:6–8]. And this is the meaning which Christ himself attached to his death when he took the cup and told the amazed disciples, 'This cup is the new covenant in my blood, even that which is poured out for you' [*Luke* 22:20]. His

willing submission to the death of the cross was a divine necessity because the mercy of God is never exercised at the expense of his righteousness [*Rom* 3:24–26]. God could only forgive the sins of his people in a manner which was consistent with his holiness [*Ps* 85:10]. Thus it took nothing less than the blood of One who was divine to make good this promise of a free pardon for guilty sinners [*Acts* 20:28]. Moreover, the non-remembrance of their sin also implies the imputation of Christ's righteousness to their account, for when God 'forgets their sins, he will have their persons in everlasting remembrance, *Ps* 112:6' (Poole). [*Rom* 5:18–21]

V13: In that he saith, A *new* covenant, he hath made the first old. But that which is becoming old and waxeth aged is nigh unto vanishing away.

By saying 'a *new* covenant,' he antiquates the first. (Moffatt) In fixing upon this one word 'new' (*kainos*) the author here stresses the superiority of that covenant which has made the former one obsolete; whereas in 12:24 he describes it as 'fresh' (*neos*) in point of time as compared with the ancient one it has replaced.

And whatever is antiquated and aged is on the verge of vanishing. (Moffatt).

If Jeremiah spoke of a 'new' covenant so long ago, how much nearer is the old order now to vanishing away! It is in a state of senile decrepitude, 'like an old, old man who is sinking into his grave. To such a thing the readers would go back if they again became Jews' (Lenski). The sacrificial system did indeed vanish away with the destruction of the temple in AD 70. 'Thus the Sinaitic superstructure became antiquated. But its foundation, the Abrahamic covenant, was never abrogated, and still stands today, as the abiding basis of the new superstructure, the new covenant' (Martin J. Wyngaarden, *The Furture of the Kingdom in Prophecy and Fulfilment*, p. 124). [*Hal* 3:15–17]

CHAPTER NINE

*The author's description of the furniture and service of the tabernacle
shows that the old covenant was a dispensation of distance. For
though the priests daily ministered in the Holy place, entrance to the
Holy of holies was barred to all, except the High Priest on the
annual Day of Atonement. And this ban proved the inadequacy of
these carnal ordinances to effect that inward purification which
would bring the worshipper near to God [vv 1–10]. But in contrast
to the High Priest's yearly entrance into the Holy of holies, Christ
once for all entered the real sanctuary of heaven in virtue of his
perfect sacrifice for sin, having obtained eternal redemption [vv
11, 12]. If then the blood of animals removed outward defilement
and gave ritual purity, how much more shall the blood of Christ,
who through his own eternal Spirit offered himself without blemish
to God, cleanse their conscience from dead works to serve the
living God? [vv 13, 14]. It is by his sacrificial death that Christ
is the Mediator of a new covenant, for the blessings of this testament
could not have been received without the death of its testator
[vv 15–17]. Thus even the provisions of the first covenant had
to be ratified by the shedding of blood, apart from which there is no
remission [vv 18–22]. But though the copies of heavenly things
required cleansing by blood, the heavenly things themselves
called for better sacrifices than these. For Christ has not entered
a holy place made with hands, but heaven itself, there to appear
before God for us. Unlike the Levitical high priest he does not*

*have to make repeated sacrifices for sin, for he has now once suffered
to put away sin by the sacrifice of himself. And as it is appointed
unto men once to die, and after this the judgment; so Christ, having
been once offered to bear the sin of many, shall appear the second
time in glory to consummate the salvation of his people [vv 23–28].*

*V*I: **Now even the first covenant had ordinances of divine service, and its sanctuary, a sanctuary of this world.**

Now the first covenant had indeed a divinely appointed
pattern of ministry and a holy place in which this service
was performed. The tabernacle which God instructed Moses
to make was a worldly sanctuary with a heavenly meaning,
but precisely because it was so firmly fixed upon the earth it
could not afford access to the heavenly reality it dimly represented [8:5].

*V*2: **For there was a tabernacle prepared, the first, wherein were the candlestick, and the table, and the showbread; which is called the Holy place.**

This tabernacle was 'made' in contrast to that which was
'not made with hands' [*v* 11]. No more is said of the tabernacle than is necessary to advance the author's argument.
He makes no mention of the outer court but simply gives a
brief description of the tent itself; the first compartment of
which was the sanctuary, or 'the Holy place,' and this con-
tained the lampstand and the table of showbread [*Exod* 25:23–
29, 37:10–24].

the candlestick (*luchnia*) Better, light-stand or lamp-stand.
W. E. Vine points out that 'candlestick' is a serious mis-
translation: 'There is no mention of a candle in the original
either in the Old Testament or in the New Testament. The
figure of that which feeds upon its own substance to provide its
light would be utterly inappropriate. A lamp is supplied by oil,
which in its symbolism is figurative of the Holy Spirit'.

*V*3: **And after the second veil, the tabernacle which is called the Holy of holies;**
*V*4: **having a golden altar of incense, and the ark of the covenant overlaid round about with gold, wherein was a golden pot holding the manna, and Aaron's rod that budded, and the tables of the covenant;**
*V*5: **and above it cherubim of glory overshadowing the mercy-seat; of which things we cannot now speak severally.**

As there was a curtain at the entrance of the sanctuary, the veil which divided this first compartment from 'the Holy of holies' is here called 'the second veil'. The 'golden altar of incense' *belonged* (cf. '*having*' with 'in which,' *v* 2) to the Holy of holies, though it was *placed* 'within the outer sanctuary in order to be daily served by the ordinary priests' (Delitzsch). [*Exod* 30:1–6, 40:5] Beyond the veil lay the ark of the covenant in which were deposited the tables of testimony, Aaron's rod that budded, and the pot with manna in it, while the mercy-seat, which formed the lid of this sacred chest, was overshadowed by the cherubim of glory [*Exod* 16:33–34, 25:16–22; *Num* 17:10]. It is not the author's intention to speak of the individual significance of these things, though doubtless he could have done so had it been within the scope of his present purpose. He chooses instead to describe what took place within this earthly tabernacle on the annual day of Atonement.

*V*6: **Now these things having been thus prepared, the priests go in continually into the first tabernacle, accomplishing the services;**
*V*7: **but into the second the high priest alone, once in the year, not without blood, which he offereth for himself, and for the errors of the people:**

Although the ordinary priests served God continually in the holy place to which they enjoyed unhindered access without blood, entrance to the inner sanctuary was forbidden to all except the high priest, but even he could enter it only once a year, and then not without the blood of sacrifice. Furthermore, 'this sacrificial blood was not finally efficacious, for fresh blood had to be shed and a fresh entry made into the holy of holies year by year' (F. F. Bruce).

As *v* 8 makes clear, the author is here contrasting the unsatisfactory service of the Levitical high priests with the complete finality of Christ's sacrifice. 'Offereth' is in the present tense to mark the fact that their work was never finished. For though the chief end of their ministry was to offer sacrifices for sins, they failed to reach the end of their task. And this was because they always brought an offering which only served to recall the sins it could not really remove [10:3, 4], whereas Christ began his priesthood by making an end of sin, and then in virtue of that sacrificial death he 'entered in once for all into the holy place, having obtained eternal redemption' [*v* 12].

Secondly, it should be noted that 'offereth' only loosely describes the high priest's function, for it is not said where or when the offering was made. But it is plain from *Lev* 16:15 that the *offering* of the sacrifice preceded the *sprinkling* of the blood upon the mercy-seat. What this indicates is that the blood secured the high priest's safe access into the holiest place; it did not provide him with the means of continuing the work of offering after entrance had thus been gained. The passage therefore provides no grounds for supposing that Christ continues 'to offer' his blood in heaven. In this Epistle his sacrificial offering is firmly located on earth [13:12], and it is repeatedly shown that this one perfect offering for sins admits of no repetition or continuation.

V 8: **the Holy Spirit this signifying, that the way into the holy place hath not yet been made manifest, while the first tabernacle is yet standing;**

By means of this restriction the Holy Spirit virtually declared that the way into the heavenly sanctuary was not open while the worship carried on in the earthly tabernacle continued in accordance with God's appointment. This period came to an end with the death of Christ, when the rending of the temple veil was the supernatural sign that at last this barrier had been removed [*Matt* 27:51]. The author does not mean that there was no experience of gospel grace under the Old Testament, but 'that unimpeded access to the presence of God was not granted until Christ came to accomplish His sacrificial ministry' (F. F. Bruce).

*V*9: **which is a figure for the time present; according to which are offered both gifts and sacrifices that cannot, as touching the conscience, make the worshipper perfect,**

That the way into the holiest was thus barred is 'a parable bearing on the present crisis' (W. Manson). It should convince the readers of the futility of returning to a system that brought nothing to perfection, for the gifts and sacrifices which were offered in connection with the earthly tabernacle could never make the worshipper complete, because in themselves they possessed no power to cleanse his conscience [cf *v* 14]. Although they sufficed to secure his ceremonial purity, they were a means of grace only insofar as they pointed forward to the final sacrifice of Christ. 'Nothing can give perfect peace of conscience with God but what can make atonement for sin. And whoever attempt it any other way but by virtue of that atonement, will never attain it, in this world nor hereafter' (John Owen).

*V*10: **being only (with meats and drinks and divers washings) carnal ordinances, imposed until a time of reformation.**

Moreover, the carnal service of the worldly sanctuary gave evidence of its provisional character, for these rites were only imposed until 'the time of the new order' (Arndt-Gingrich). [*Acts* 15:10] The arrival of the promised Seed meant that those who still rashly continued to observe these ordinances did so without a divine warrant and in consequence were left with nothing but the empty husks of a superseded ritual.

*V*11: **But Christ having come a high priest of the good things to come, through the greater and more perfect tabernacle, not made with hands, that is to say, not of this creation,**

But when Christ appeared as a high priest of the good things that have come, (RSV) This better reading is in line with the 'realized eschatology' of the author. For though believers are still pilgrims on their way to Zion [11:16], spiritually speaking they have already arrived [12:22–24]! The present possession of these heavenly blessings was secured 'through' the triumphant entrance of our great high priest into that sanctuary which is not of this world because it is 'not made with hands' [*Acts* 7:48, 17:24]. The official designation 'Christ' not only draws attention to the Messianic fulfilment of what was typified in the material copy, but also indicates the representative nature of his entry into heaven by which the salvation of his people is assured. For God's acceptance of the person of the Mediator is the indisputable proof of the efficacy of the sacrifice he had offered on their behalf [8:3]. As P. E. Hughes explains, the reason that 'tabernacle' and 'the holy place' [*v* 12] are treated as synonymous terms is because the veil which divided the earthly tent into two chambers has been abolished by Christ's death [*v* 8]. *Thus Christ entered the true tabernacle (of heaven) which is the true sanctuary (of God's presence).*

*V*12: **nor yet through the blood of goats and calves, but through his own blood, entered in once for all into the holy place, having obtained eternal redemption.**

[116]

As the opening disclaimer shows, Christ not only ministers in a better place [v 11], he also offered a better sacrifice. The blood of goats and calves brought the Levitical high priest only once a year into the holy place of the earthly tabernacle, but it was 'through his own blood' that Christ entered 'once for all' into heaven itself. H. C. G. Moule correctly states, 'Blood *shed* is not a vehicle of power, but an evidence of death, especially by sacrifice or execution'. So what these high priests had in common was that they both entered a sanctuary in virtue of a sacrificial death. To give evidence of that death the earthly high priest took *with him* the blood of another victim, but as Christ was both priest and sacrifice he presented only *himself*! 'His "entering in" as the Crucified One Risen *is* the presentation' (Moule, *Outlines of Christian Doctrine*, pp. 85, 105).

Christ thus 'entered in not with, but "through his own blood," that is, by means of, or because of, His death as Man, when His human blood was shed. So, in the heavenly glory, He does not sprinkle, and never has actually sprinkled, blood upon some heavenly mercy-seat' (A. M. Stibbs, *The Meaning of the Word 'Blood' in Scripture*, p. 18). The remarks of John Owen on the verse are to the same effect: 'It is a vain speculation, contrary to the analogy of faith, and destructive of the true nature of the oblation of Christ, and inconsistent with the dignity of his person, that he should carry with him into heaven a part of that material blood which was shed for us on the earth. This some have invented, to maintain a comparison in that wherein is none intended. The design of the apostle is only to declare by virtue of what he entered as a priest into the holy place. And this was by virtue of his own blood when it was shed, when he offered himself unto God'. Yet it is this unscriptural idea which is given support by the RSV, 'taking . . . his own blood', an inexcusable inaccuracy which is justly criticized by both F. F. Bruce and T. Hewitt.

having obtained eternal redemption. What Christ obtained by his death was *eternal* redemption in contrast with the *temporary* deliverance effected by the Levitical sacrifices. As these sacrifices sufficed for all who were represented by the earthly high priest, so the sacrifice of Christ actually saves all who are included within the scope of his work. He did not die to secure a mere possible redemption of all men, but purposely 'to give his life a ransom *for many*' [*Mark* 10:45]. 'It is to beggar the concept of redemption as an effective securement of release by price and by power to construe it as anything less than the effectual accomplishment which secures the salvation of those who are its objects. Christ did not come to put men in a redeemable position but to redeem to himself a people' (John Murray, *Redemption Accomplished and Applied*, p. 63).

*V*13: **For if the blood of goats and bulls, and the ashes of a heifer sprinkling them that have been defiled, sanctify unto the cleanness of the flesh:**

This justifies the preceding affirmation [*v* 12]: 'For if the blood sacrifices of the tabernacle served to purify the *flesh* from ceremonial uncleanness, then how much more shall the blood of Christ cleanse the *conscience* from dead works to serve the living God?' The defilement produced by physical contact with a dead body excluded the person affected from the congregation of Israel, but the sprinkling of the ashes of an heifer provide a ritual cleansing which again fitted him to join in the worship of God [*Num* 19]. 'The spiritual Israelite derived, in these legal rites, spiritual blessings not flowing from them, but from the Antitype. Ceremonial sacrifices released from *temporal penalties* and *ceremonial disqualifications:* Christ's sacrifice releases from *everlasting penalties* [*v* 12] and *moral impurities of conscience* disqualifying from access to God [*v* 14]' (Fausset).

*V*14: **how much more shall the blood of Christ, who through the eternal Spirit offered himself without blemish unto God, cleanse your conscience from dead works to serve the living God?**

If therefore even the blood of animals sufficed to secure such an external purification, how much more shall the blood of Christ effect the moral cleansing of the conscience?

> *Not all the blood of beasts,*
> *On Jewish altars slain,*
> *Could give the guilty conscience peace,*
> *Or wash away the stain.*
>
> *But Christ, the heavenly Lamb,*
> *Takes all our sins away;*
> *A sacrifice of nobler Name,*
> *And richer blood than they.*
>
> (Isaac Watts)

who through his eternal spirit offered himself (ASV margin) This means that 'in virtue of his inseparable and unchangeable Divine Nature Christ was Priest while he was victim also' (Westcott). In other words, that which gave Christ's sacrifice its atoning value was the *voluntary* character of that act, for he was at once 'the sacrificing Priest' and 'the sacrificed Lamb' (Lenski). And because he made the offering through his *eternal* spirit, which could not be extinguished by death (cf 7:16: 'the power of a life that cannot be destroyed' – NEB), he entered heaven once-for-all 'having obtained *eternal* redemption' [*v* 12]. Thus the reference is not to the Holy Spirit, 'but to the Spirit which was His own, that is, to *Christ's divine nature*. Also, the word *eternal* here means *heavenly*. Therefore the meaning is that *through the heavenly aspect of His deity* Christ makes the offering. This is also borne out by the opening words of the Epistle:"...the Son, after he had made propitiation of sins in himself". The verb here is in the middle voice, which is significant, indicating something taking place *within Christ's Person*' (Vos).

without blemish unto God, The efficacy of the Levitical offerings depended upon the outward perfection of the sacrifice, but what Christ offered to God was *Himself*, an offering without inward blemish or moral impurity of any kind [1 *Pet* 1:19].

cleanse your conscience from dead works to serve the living God? 'We must note the aim of atonement, which is *to serve the living God*. We are not cleansed by Christ so that we can immerse ourselves continually in fresh dirt, but in order that our purity may serve the glory of God. He [the author of Hebrews] goes on to say that nothing can proceed from us which is pleasing to God until we are cleansed by the blood of Christ. Since we are all enemies of God before our reconciliation, all that we do is likewise hateful to Him. The beginning of true worship is therefore reconciliation. Because no work is so pure or free from sin as to be pleasing to God by itself, cleansing by the blood of Christ which destroys all stains must necessarily intervene. This is the true contrast between the living God and dead works' (Calvin).

V15: **And for this cause he is the mediator of a new covenant, that a death having taken place for the redemption of the transgressions that were under the first covenant, they that have been called may receive the promise of the eternal inheritance.**

It is on account of the infinite superiority of his sacrifice that Christ is the Mediator of the new 'covenant' (the same word, *diathēkē*, is used in *vv* 16, 17 in the sense of a 'testament'). The old covenant extended a promise of eternal life, but it was unable to confer it, for the blood of animals could never provide a real atonement for sin. As therefore nothing less than the death of Christ could cancel the guilt of those 'called' in the former dispensation, Christians of New Testament days had no reason to be offended by it; for *all* who receive the 'eternal' inheritance do so in virtue of that 'eternal' redemption [*v* 12] which was obtained by means of Christ's 'eternal' spirit [*v* 14]. Thus the real value in the typical sacrifices of the old covenant is found in the one perfect sacrifice to which they pointed. 'It is Christ's death that gives worth to the types that pointed to him. So then the atoning sacrifice of Christ is the basis of the salvation of all who are saved before the Cross and since' (Robertson).

*V*16: **For where a testament is, there must of necessity be the death of him that made it.**
*V*17: **For a testament is of force where there hath been death: for it doth never avail while he that made it liveth.**

Having mentioned a 'death' and an 'inheritance' in the previous verse, the author here slides easily into the second meaning of *diathēkē* as a 'last will and testament'. It has been pointed out that this change of meaning appeared so natural to the Greek commentators on this Epistle that they make no remark on it. 'There is no more possibility or feasibility of interference with the effective application of the blessings of the covenant than there is of interfering with a testamentary disponement (or disposition) once the testator has died. This use of the testamentary provision of Roman law to illustrate the inviolable security accruing from the sacrificial death of Christ serves to underline the unilateral character of the new covenant. One thing is apparent, that a testament is a unilateral disposition of possession. How totally foreign to the notion of compact, contract, or agreement is the disposition or dispensation which can be illustrated in respect of its effective operation by a last will!' (John Murray, *The Covenant of Grace*, p. 30).

*V*18: **Wherefore even the first covenant hath not been dedicated without blood.**

In this verse the reference to the blood of sacrifice shows that the author reverts to the concept of a 'covenant.' Those who were tempted to look askance at the blood of Christ are here reminded that the Sinaitic covenant was not inaugurated without the shedding of blood [*Exod* 24:3–8].

*V*19: **For when every commandment had been spoken by Moses unto all the people according to the law, he took the blood of the calves and the goats, with water and scarlet wool and hyssop, and sprinkled both the book itself and all the people,**
*V*20: **saying, This is the blood of the covenant which God commanded to you-ward.**

Several details in this description are not found in the Exodus narrative but though the sources used by the author are no longer available for our scrutiny we are not thereby obliged to doubt the accuracy of his inspired account of the matter [2 *Tim* 3:16]. What he wishes to emphasize is that all the provisions of that covenant were solemnly ratified by Moses when he sprinkled both the book and the people with the blood which he then identified as 'the blood of the covenant'.

*V*21: **Moreover the tabernacle and all the vessels of the ministry he sprinkled in like manner with the blood.**

Subsequently even the tabernacle itself and all its sacred vessels required to be cleansed by blood so that they might be used by sinners without receiving defilement from them [*Lev*] 16:14–20].

*V*22: **And according to the law, I may almost say, all things are cleansed with blood, and apart from shedding of blood there is no remission.**

In fact under the law 'I may almost say, all things are cleansed with blood,' without which 'there is no remission'. Although those who could only afford a bloodless offering still obtained remission, such exceptions nevertheless derived their efficacy from the universal rule on which they were based [*Lev* 5:11–13]. The author's insistence upon this principle makes it hard to see how there can be any remission of sins granted through the 'unbloody' offering of the mass. 'There is in the mass no real Christ, no suffering, and no bleeding. And a bloodless sacrifice is ineffectual. The writer of the book of Hebrews says that "apart from shedding of blood there is no remission" of sin [9:22]; and John says, "The blood of Jesus his Son cleanseth us from all sin" [1 *John* 1:7]. Since admittedly there is no blood in the mass, it simply cannot be a sacrifice for sin' (L. Boettner, *Roman Catholicism*, p. 227). This is therefore an unscriptural practice which 'dishonours and degrades the one perfect and all-sufficient sacrifice of Christ, by representing it as repeated, or rather caricatured, daily and hourly by the juggling mummery of a priest' (William Cunningham, *Historical Theology*, Vol. II, p. 143).

*V*23: **It was necessary therefore that the copies of the things in the heavens should be cleansed with these; but the heavenly things themselves with better sacrifices than these.**

But while such animal sacrifices sufficed to cleanse the earthly sanctuary, 'better sacrifices' than these were needed to purify heaven for man's entrance. This plural is used because the verse states only the general principle, though presently it will be shown that this access into God's presence was effected by 'one sacrifice' [10:12]. 'The earthly tabernacle, as God's dwelling, might have been supposed to be hallowed by his presence and to need no cleansing, but being also his meeting-place with men it required to be cleansed. And so our heavenly relations with God, and all wherewith we seek to approach him, need cleansing. In themselves things heavenly need no cleansing, but as entered upon by sinful men they need it. Our eternal relations with God require purification' (Marcus Dods).

V24: **For Christ entered not into a holy place made with hands, like in pattern to the true; but into heaven itself, now to appear before the face of God for us:**

Christ therefore has not entered a holy place made with hands which was but a copy of the celestial reality, but has appeared in heaven itself as the representative of a people who now enjoy through him continuous and unrestricted access into the very presence of God. 'It is enough that Jesus should *show himself for us* to the Father: the sight of Jesus satisfied God in our behalf. He brings before the face of God no offering which has exhausted itself, and, as only sufficing for a time, needs renewal; but he himself is in person, by virtue of the eternal Spirit, i.e., the imperishable life of his person, now and for ever freed from death, our eternally-present offering before God' (Delitzsch).

V25: **nor yet that he should offer himself often, as the high priest entereth into the holy place year by year with blood not his own;**

Unlike the Levitical high priest who entered the holy place each year 'with blood not his own', Christ made the unrepeatable offering of his own blood through which he entered into the heavenly sanctuary once-for-all. 'Whatever had the greatest glory in the old legal institutions, carried along with it the evidence of its own imperfection, compared with the thing signified in Christ and his office. – The entrance of the high priest into the holy place was the most glorious solemnity of the law; howbeit the annual repetition of it was a sufficient evidence of its imperfection' (John Owen).

*V*26: **else must he often have suffered since the foundation of the world: but now once at the end of the ages
hath he been manifested to put away sin by the sacrifice
of himself.**

The sufficiency of this offering is proved by its finality; for
if its benefits did not extend to former generations [*v* 15],
then Christ must have suffered repeatedly from the time
that man first became a sinner. But since he did not so suffer,
it is evident that he made a complete offering for the sins
of his people. For *He* did not painlessly present the blood
of others but offered *Himself*, and this entailed mortal suffering
which clearly cannot be repeated. Hence those who presume
to present this offering anew have fallen back to the level
of a superseded priesthood! For true Christian worship
leaves the sacrifice where 'God the Lord of time placed it – at
that exact historical moment in the third decade of our
chronology. It is the saving consequences of that atoning
act, not the act itself, which become a present event in our
worship' (Oscar Cullmann, *The Christology of the New
Testament*, p. 99).

**but now once at the end of the ages hath he been mani-
fested to put away sin by the sacrifice of himself.** But now
that Christ has been historically manifested he has annulled
sin's power by exhausting its penalty in his priestly self-
oblation upon the cross. 'At the end of the ages' marks the
end of the period of preparation. Since God had determined
that there was to be one sacrifice for all generations, the occur-
rence of that sacrifice marked the beginning of the age to
come, and closed the period of symbolism and expectation.

*V*27: **And inasmuch as it is appointed unto men once to
die, and after this cometh judgment;**
*V*28: **so Christ also, having been once offered to bear**

**the sins of many, shall appear a second time, apart from
sin, to them that wait for him, unto salvation.**

The author appeals to the universal fact of death to confirm
his statement that Christ's death was 'once for all'. 'Man dies
once, and the next thing before him is judgment. So Christ
died once and the next thing before him is the Advent'
(Vaughan). Death became a divine appointment for man
through his one primal act of disobedience, and the judgment
which must follow it registers the unfavourable verdict
of God upon a sinful life. Such a verdict could only be reversed
through a vicarious satisfaction for sin, and this Christ
accomplished in accordance with the prophecy of Isaiah
(cf 53:12: 'he bare the sin of many'). The dreadful anguish
with which Cardinal Newman's Gerontius faced the Great
Assize is in startling contrast to the New Testament which
speaks of the believer's 'boldness in the day of judgment'
[1 John 4:17]. Plainly this is not a presumptuous confidence,
for the assurance of his complete absolution from all guilt
is based upon the full satisfaction which Christ made for his
sin. It is to be further noted that the extent of the atonement
is determined by the number who are finally saved by it.
The passage represents the second advent of Christ, this time
without even the imputation of sin, as the climactic event
which will consummate the salvation of 'the many' for whom
he once suffered.

'It is the great exercise of faith, to live on the invisible act-
ings of Christ on the behalf of the church. So also the foundation of it doth consist in our infallible expectation of his
second appearance, of our seeing him again, Acts 1:11. . .The
present long-continued absence of Christ in heaven is the
great trial of the world. God doth give the world *a trial
by faith in Christ*, as he gave it *a trial by obedience in Adam*.
Faith is tried by difficulties. When Christ did appear, it was
under such circumstances as turned all unbelievers from him.
His state was then a state of infirmity, reproach, and suffering.

He appeared in the flesh. Now he is in glory, he appeareth not. As many refused him when he appeared, because it was in outward weakness; so many refuse him now he is in glory, because he appeareth not. Faith alone can conflict with and conquer these difficulties' (John Owen). [*Rev* 22:20]

CHAPTER TEN

In summing up his argument, the author points out that the repeated sacrifices prescribed by the law only served to remind the people of their sinfulness, for it is impossible that the blood of animals should take away sins [vv 1–4]. As foretold by the Psalmist, this great lack was supplied when Christ came into the world to sanctify his people through the once-for-all offering of his own body on their behalf [vv 5–10]. For whereas the Levitical priests daily stand to offer those sacrifices which can never take away sins, Christ sat down on the right hand of God after he had offered the one perfect sacrifice for sins, having thus secured the complete reinstatement of his people in accordance with Jeremiah's prophecy of the new covenant [vv 11–18]. Therefore as Christ has opened up a new and living way to God, let us boldly enter the holy place through the redeeming merit of our great Priest [vv 19–22]. Let us hold fast our confession, and encourage one another, not forsaking the assembling together for worship as the day of the Lord's return draws near [vv 23–25]. Waverers are again solemnly warned that if they wilfully renounce their interest in Christ, they will incur a judgment far more severe than that which overtook the despisers of the law, as befits those who have trampled under foot the Son of God himself [vv 26–31]. Let them recall the former days of faith, when they joyfully endured much persecution, so that they do not now cast away the prospect of their reward. Let us then remember our identity: we are not of those who shrink back to perdition, but of those who have faith to the saving of the soul [vv 32–39].

*V*1: **For the law having a shadow of the good things to come, not the very image of the things, can never with the same sacrifices year by year, which they offer continually, make perfect them that draw nigh.**

Having proved the finality of Christ's sacrifice, the author next insists upon its perfection. He begins by conceding that the law had indeed a shadow of the good things to come, but a shadow could never fulfil the expectations to which it gave rise. But at last this unsubstantial promise had given place to the very image itself, for the new age which was inaugurated by the finished work of Christ 'is not merely a reproduction of the Heavenly Reality, but its actual substance, the Reality itself come down from heaven' (Vos). Thus the law could never make perfect those who sought to draw near to God through the continuous succession of sacrifices which it prescribed, and this was because 'no repetition of the shadow can amount to the substance' (A. B. Davidson).

*V*2: **Else would they not have ceased to be offered? because the worshippers, having been once cleansed, would have had no more consciousness of sins.**

The question summons the readers to reflect on the significance of these repeated offerings, for if any one of them had been adequate to pacify the consciences of the worshippers by effecting a real purification of sins then this would have brought the series to an end. The impotence of these offerings is therefore self-confessed. The argument used here suggests that the Epistle was written before AD 70 when the destruction of the temple ensured the cessation of all sacrifices. 'All peace with God is resolved into a purging atonement made for sin: "Being once purged"' (John Owen).

V3: **But in those sacrifices there is a remembrance made of sins year by year.**

'It would not have occurred to an observant Jew under the Mosaic covenant to say that the Day of Atonement involved an annual "remembrance" of sins; he would have said, rather, that there was an annual *removal* of sins. Our author might have replied, truly enough, that the ritual designed to effect the removal of sins necessarily involves their remembrance; but he is influenced chiefly by the promise that under the new covenant God will remember His people's sins no more. Since the new covenant is contrasted with the old, the implication is that there was no such absolute wiping out of sins from the divine record under the sacrificial law' (F. F. Bruce).

V4: **For it is impossible that the blood of bulls and goats should take away sins.**

He does not deal here with the positive value of what had been a divine appointment, but only shows what these sacrifices could not do when considered in themselves. This trenchant judgment was timely, for to forsake Christ in order to return to a system of worship that had outlived its usefulness, would amount to an accounting of 'the precious blood of Christ'as inferior in value to the blood of beasts which could never take away sin. 'This obvious truth needs no proof. There is no relation between the physical blood of animals and man's moral offence' (Marcus Dods).

V5: **Wherefore when he cometh into the world, he saith,**

> **Sacrifice and offering thou wouldest not,**
> **But a body didst thou prepare for me;**

V6:   **In whole burnt offerings and sacrifices for sin thou hadst no pleasure:**

V7:   **Then said I, Lo, I am come**

(In the roll of the book it is written of me)
To do thy will, O God.

The author sees a prophetic anticipation of the whole earthly course of Christ in the words uttered by David in *Ps* 40:6-8. 'It is not as if Christ, and *not* David, were the speaker: David speaks; but Christ, whose Spirit already dwells and works in David, and who will hereafter receive from David His human nature, now already speaks *in* him' (Delitzsch).

Sacrifice and offering thou wouldest not This is not a rejection of sacrifices as such; it rather affirms the common prophetic doctrine that ritual offerings are worthless without corresponding obedience of heart and life [cf *Mic* 6:6-8; 1 *Sam* 15:22; *Ps* 50:8-14, 51:16f; *Is* 1:11f; *Jer* 7:21f; *Hos* 6:6; *Amos* 5:21f]. What is new here is David's inspired recognition of the fact that sacrifices cannot adequately express his devotion to God, and so he speaks 'as if his self-offering will be the sacrifice to end all sacrifices' (Derek Kidner). The sacred rhetoric of David thus prophetically points forward to the only One who could bring it to fulfilment.

But a body didst thou prepare for me The quotation follows the Greek version of the Psalm, and Lenski suggests that its substitution of 'a body didst thou prepare for me' for the Hebrew 'mine ears hast thou digged' (AV margin) was due to the desire of the translators to make it more intelligible to Greek readers. In either case, there is no material difference in meaning, for attentive hearing prepares for obedient service [*Is* 50:4-7]. And it was Christ's voluntary submission to the will of God which distinguished the offering of his body from the forced and non-rational offering of the bodies of beasts in sacrifice. As E. Schweizer points out, This emphasis on the fact that Jesus consciously offered up his body in sacrifice is a new use [*vv* 5, 10], for elsewhere 'body' is practically never used in the vocabulary of sacrifice (*TDNT*, Vol. vii, p. 1058).

Then said I, Lo, I am come. . .to do thy will, O God
The language vividly expresses the eager promptitude of
Christ's complete dedication to the will of God. 'There is
nothing of irresponsibility or adventure in Christ's life and
death. It is all obedience, and therefore it is all revelation.
We see God in it because it is not His own will but the will
of the Father which it accomplished. Even when we come
to consider its relation to sin, this must be borne in mind.
Atonement is not something contrived, as it were, behind
the Father's back; it is the Father's way of making it possible
for the sinful to have fellowship with Him' (James Denney,
The Death of Christ, p. 122).

*V*8: **Saying above, Sacrifices and offerings and whole
burnt offerings and sacrifices for sin thou wouldest
not, neither hadst pleasure therein (the which are offered
according to the law),**
*V*9: **then hath he said, Lo, I am come to do thy will.
He taketh away the first, that he may establish the
second.**

These words of the Messiah therefore show that God's dis-
satisfaction with the sacrifices which were offered according
to the law pointed forward to their replacement by his
own perfect obedience to the divine will. Hence the abrogation of the first must mean the establishment of the second:
so that those who continue to offer such sacrifices, whether
animal or material (as opposed to the spiritual 'sacrifices'
of 13:16; *Rom* 12:1, 2), after Christ's definitive sacrifice
are guilty of the sin of flagrant opposition to the will of God!

*V*10: **By which will we have been sanctified through
the offering of the body of Jesus Christ once for all.**

'The will of God, with which we are here concerned, is not
satisfied by an obedience which comes short of death. For it is
not merely the preceptive will of God, His will that men

[132]

should do right and live according to His holy law, which Christ came to fulfil; it is His gracious will, a will which has as its aim that sinful men should be constituted into a people for Himself, a will which has resolved that their sin should be so dealt with as no longer to keep them at a distance from Him; a will, in short, that sinners should find a standing in His sight. And in that will we are sanctified, not merely by Christ's fulfilment of the law of God as it is binding on man in general, but by His fulfilment of the law as it is binding on sinful men, by His obedient suffering of death as that in which God's mind in relation to sin finds its final expression' (James Denney).

once for all. That which has been completed *for* the believer obviously cannot refer to a gradual process *within* the believer. Accordingly, this 'sanctification' is the objective achievement of Christ which has secured the purification of his people and for ever set them apart for the service of God. It has a forensic import which is analogous to the Pauline concept of 'justification'.

*V*11: **And every priest indeed standeth day by day ministering and offering oftentimes the same sacrifices, the which can never take away sins:**
*V*12: **but he, when he had offered one sacrifice for sins for ever, sat down on the right hand of God;**
*V*13: **henceforth expecting till his enemies be made the footstool of his feet.**

The Levitical priests must *stand* as they daily offer the very same sacrifices which can never take away sins. But this Priest after he had offered one sacrifice for sins for ever, *sat down* on the right hand of God [1:3]. Christ's heavenly enthronement bears witness to the eternal validity of that one historic sacrifice by which he made reconciliation for iniquity and brought in everlasting righteousness [*Dan* 9:24].

The author's intention in echoing the word of *Ps* 110:1 in *v* 13 is probably to warn the readers 'not to let themselves be numbered among the enemies of the exalted Christ, but rather to be reckoned as His friends and companions by preserving their fidelity to the end' (F. F. Bruce). [3:14, 10:26–31]

*V*14: **For by one offering he hath perfected for ever them that are sanctified.**

This verse rules out the possibility of any further offering for sins either on earth or in heaven, for it affirms that Christ has perfected for ever those who are consecrated to God by his *one* offering on their behalf. According to John Flavel this means, 'that the oblation made unto God by Jesus Christ, is of unspeakable value, and everlasting efficacy, to perfect all them that are, or shall be sanctified, to the end of the world' (*Works*, Vol. I, p. 155).

*V*15: **And the Holy Spirit also beareth witness to us; for after he hath said,**
*V*16: **This is the covenant that I will make with them**
    After those days, saith the Lord:
    I will put my laws on their heart,
    And upon their mind also will I write them;
then saith he,
*V*17: **And their sins and their iniquities will I remember**
    no more.
*V*18: **Now where remission of these is, there is no more offering for sin.**

Earlier in the Epistle [8:8f] the author had drawn the attention of his readers to the newness of that covenant which had made the first old, but here he appeals once more to this testimony of the Holy Spirit in order to underline its finality [*Jer* 31: 31f]. God's promise that he will no more remember the sins of his people is the outstanding feature of the new covenant, for the continual remembrance of sins under the old economy showed the insufficiency of its constant sacrifices to atone for sin [v 3]. But Christ blotted out the sins of his people beyond recall when he offered himself to God on their behalf. His death ratified the new covenant and abolished the old order. Thus where there is the full remission of sins, no possibility of any further offering for sin remains. The author's emphatic reiteration of this truth was necessary for those who were thinking of going back to Judaism and all its sacrifices, but it must be noted that the general character of his final word includes every kind of supposed offering for sin. For since Christ's sacrifice all other sacrifices for sin are utterly futile and meaningless.

V19: **Having therefore, brethren, boldness to enter into the holy place by the blood of Jesus,**

Exposition now gives place to exhortation, and the remainder of the Epistle is devoted to a detailed application of the eloquent appeal which begins in this verse and extends to v 25. He addresses his readers as 'brethren' to remind them of the privileges which are inseparable from their profession of faith in Christ, for it is as those who realize that their acceptance by God rests entirely upon the sacrificial death of their great High Priest that he bids them boldly to enter the heavenly sanctuary. 'Christians do not enter the holiest *with* the blood of Jesus, for then they would be priests, anew opening up the way, whenever they approached, by a new offering; the view of the passage is that the way is opened up once for all by the offering of the Son [9:12, 28; 10:12], and lies for ever open because He abides before the face of God for us [9:24]; and it is on this fact, called here the blood of Jesus, that the glad confidence of believers in regard to entrance is based' (A. B. Davidson).

V20: **by the way which he dedicated for us, a new and living way, through the veil, that is to say, his flesh;**

This entering into the presence of God is by that fresh and living way which Jesus has *inaugurated* by his sacrifice, for the veil barred man's access to 'the holy place' until *he* opened up the way. The Old Testament way into the sanctuary 'was simply a lifeless pavement trodden by the high priest, and by him alone' (Delitzsch); whereas the 'living way' is of vital and perpetual efficacy because the *living* and *life-giving* Saviour is that way [7:25].

through the veil, that is to say, his flesh; As there was no way into the inner sanctuary of the tabernacle except through the veil, so the flesh of Jesus affords the only means of access to the heavenly sanctuary [*Mark* 15:38]. 'The crucified Christ is the entrance, the entrance veil. "No man cometh to the Father but *by me*", *John* 14:6, by my blood, by my flesh, by this veil. This veil shuts out and forever hides the Father from all those who spurn it as the means of entry' (Lenski).

*V*21: **and having a great priest over the house of God;**

This further reminder of the greatness of the Priest who now presides over the house of God is designed to encourage their confident approach to the throne of grace, and also to warn them against any return to the ministrations of a discarded priesthood. 'Christ could not be a high priest unless the former priests were divested of their office, since theirs was a different order. He means therefore that all those things which Christ changed at His coming are to be let go. He sets Him over the whole house of God so that whoever wishes to have a place in the Church must submit to Christ and choose Him and no other as his leader and ruler' (Calvin). [3:1–6, 4:14–16]

*V*22: **let us draw near with a true heart in fulness of faith, having our hearts sprinkled from an evil conscience: and having our body washed with pure water,**

It is in virtue of Christ's one offering for sin and the perfection of his priesthood that they are exhorted to draw near [cf comment on 4:16] to God 'with a true heart in full assurance of faith' (AV). These are the prime requisites in every approach to God: *sincerity of heart*, because he desires 'truth in the inward parts' and hates all hypocrisy, falsehood, and deceit [*Ps* 51:6; *John* 4:24]; *full assurance of faith*, because 'he that cometh to God must believe that he is, and that he is a rewarder of them that seek after him' [11:6].

having had our hearts sprinkled from an evil conscience and having had our bodies washed with pure water.
(Wuest) As these perfect participles point to unrepeatable acts with abiding effects, they 'express not conditions of approach to God which are yet to be achieved, but conditions already possessed' (Marcus Dods). This cultic language recalls the purification which the Levitical priests had to undergo before they were fit to approach God [cf *Exod* 29:4, 21], but the author evidently pours a Christian content into these terms. In effect he is saying, 'We believers have experienced through the death of Christ that once-for-all *inward cleansing* from sin which was given its *outward expression* in our baptism'. Thus the Christian's subjective confidence [*v* 22a] must always be based upon his personal interest in Christ's objective work [*v* 22b].

*V*23: **let us hold fast the confession of our hope that it waver not; for he is faithful that promised:**

Since the author knows that the Christian's confidence in the promise is best sustained by a firm conviction of the reliability of the Promiser, he reinforces this call to continue in the faith by reminding his readers that the attainment of the hope they had confessed is based on the unchanging faithfulness of God [11:11; I *Cor* 1:9; I *Thess* 5:24]. Perseverance is the hallmark of a genuine interest in Christ, but inconstancy imperils the eternal inheritance, for the hope of salvation is liable to wither when the frank confession of it wavers.

*V*24: **and let us consider one another to provoke unto love and good works;**

In place of the selfish individualism which only fosters strife, they must constantly seek to encourage and edify one another by those deeds of love which will express the reality of their fellowship in Christ. The professing church today sorely stands in need of a renewal of such 'provocations' ! [*Phil* 2:1–5] It is worth noting that 'love' here completes the familiar triad of Christian virtues ('faith', *v* 22; 'hope', *v* 23; 'love', *v* 24; cf 1 *Cor* 13:13 and 1 *Thess* 1:3).

*V*25: **not forsaking our own assembling together, as the custom of some is, but exhorting one another; and so much the more, as ye see the day drawing nigh.**

It is because the New Testament knows nothing of a solitary Christianity that the author presses upon his readers the duty of assembling together for worship, instruction, and mutual encouragement. Even if it is not welcome, this warning is nevertheless necessary for their spiritual welfare, as the partial neglect of the means of grace is the first step towards a total decline from grace. Indeed the sluggishness of some should rather serve to quicken them to greater diligence in the encouragement of one another, and all the more so as they see 'the day drawing nigh'. The early church did not consider the second advent of Christ to be an interesting topic for cold chronological calculation, for it lived in the earnest expectation of that momentous event [*Rev* 22:20]. The actual situation which this verse reflects is beyond our ken, but it seems likely that the letter was sent in the first place to Jewish Christians in Rome, some of whom were leaving the meetings of the church and contemplating a return to the Jewish synagogues to avoid further persecution [*vv* 32–34].

*V*26: **For if we sin wilfully after that we have received the knowledge of the truth, there remaineth no more a sacrifice for sins,**

As under the law there was no forgiveness of deliberate sin, sin committed 'with a high hand' [*Num* 15:30; AV margin] so under the gospel there is no provision for the reinstatement of those who wilfully fall away from their profession of faith in Christ. Both classes of sinners are worthy of the same sentence of death, for both are guilty of rejecting God's 'covenant' outside of which there is no salvation [*v* 29]. Hence the sternness of the author's warning matches the wickedness of the sin. He shows his readers the awful doom that awaits apostates on the day of judgment [*v* 27f], in order that they might realize the consequences of severing their connection with Christ by a permanent withdrawal from the Christian assembly [*v* 25; cf 1 *John* 2:19]. What we have here is a dreadful disclosure of the fate which must inevitably overtake anyone who, after having professed an interest in Christ's salvation, then deliberately and defiantly repudiates it. This settled *state* of rebellion against the gospel is not to be confused with isolated *acts* of sin which may be committed through weakness or ignorance. The warning of 6:4–8 has the same sin in view, but there the psychological aspect is stressed: the fact that repentance and renewal is impossible. Here the emphasis is linked with God's terms of salvation: there is no sacrifice to wipe out this sin.

there remaineth no more a sacrifice for sins, It is because Christ's sacrifice is the only sacrifice for sin, that the man who wilfully rejects that sacrifice in order to return to the dead works and lifeless service of Judaism, finds that there is no other sacrifice for sin to which he can have recourse.

*V*27: **but a certain fearful expectation of judgment, and a fierceness of fire which shall devour the adversaries.**

Having spurned the sacrifice of Christ, there remains for the apostate only a fearful expectation of the furious fire of divine judgment which is to devour the adversaries [12:29; *Rev* 21:8]. The word 'certain' indicates a punishment of 'undefined, undefinable magnitude – something that is inexpressible, inconceivable . . . The most dreadful conception comes infinitely short of the more dreadful reality. We can only say of it, "It is a certain fearful punishment which the apostate has to expect" ' (John Brown).

*V*28: **A man that hath set at nought Moses' law dieth without compassion on the word of two or three witnesses:**
*V*29: **of how much sorer punishment, think ye, shall he be judged worthy, who hath trodden under foot the Son of God, and hath counted the blood of the covenant wherewith he was sanctified an unholy thing, and hath done despite unto the Spirit of grace?**

The equity of the judgment is vindicated by the enormity of the offence, for if the person who set at nought the law of Moses was punished without mercy, then it is evident that the sin of one who is guilty of despising the Son must be visited with far greater severity [*Deut* 17:2-7]. This sin is unpardonable because a contemptuous rejection of the gospel is nothing less than a trampling under foot of the Son of God, a profanation of the blood of the new covenant, and a scorning of the Spirit of grace.

the blood . . . wherewith he was sanctified Although the apostate never was regenerate he was once externally dedicated to God by a profession of faith in Christ's atoning blood, and it was from this alone that he fell away. John Murray states that there is a certain sense in which it can be said that Christ died for the non-elect, but the benefits which they derive from the atonement are only temporary. 'The difference can be stated bluntly to be that the non-elect do not participate in the benefits *of* the atonement and the elect do. The non-elect enjoy many benefits that accrue *from* the atonement but they do not partake of the *atonement*' (*Collected Writings*, Vol. I, pp. 64–69).

*V*30: **For we know him that said, Vengeance belongeth unto me, I will recompense. And again, The Lord shall judge his people.**

The author now appeals to the Hebrew Christians' own knowledge of the absolute rectitude of the Judge as he introduces two quotations which confirm the righteousness of the sentence which is to be executed upon all such despisers of the gospel. 'It is a most profitable exercise for the soul to be often engaged in contemplating the Divine attributes, pondering God's almighty power, ineffable holiness, unimpeachable veracity, exact justice, absolute faithfulness and terrible severity. Christ Himself has bidden us "fear Him which is able to destroy both soul and body in hell" [*Matt* 10:28]. The better God's character be known, the more we heed that exhortation of Christ's, the clearer shall we perceive that there is nothing unsuited to the holiness of God in what Scripture affirms concerning His dealings with the wicked. It is because the true nature of sin is so little viewed in the light of God's awful holiness, that so many fail to recognize its *infinite* demerits' (A. W. Pink).

Vengeance belongeth unto me, I will recompense. Both quotations are from the Song of Moses. The first, *Deut* 32:35, appears in the version followed by Paul in *Rom* 12:19. Although in their original setting these words refer to the vengeance which will overtake the enemies of Israel, they state a principle of universal application, for as John Trapp tersely remarks, 'If God will avenge his elect, *Luke* 18:7, how much more his Son and his Spirit!'

And again, The Lord shall judge his people. This is taken from the next verse, *Deut* 32:36, where the words mean that the Lord will do judgment *for* his people, i.e. in the sense of vindicating them. Here they are quoted to show that those who forsake his covenant cannot expect to escape his righteous judgment, for when greater privileges are lightly esteemed heavier judgment is incurred [cf *Amos* 3:2].

*V*31: **It is a fearful thing to fall into the hands of the living God.**

The dumb idols of the heathen could neither help nor punish their self-deceived devotees, but because Israel's God *lives* he has the power to fulfil every promise and to make his threatened judgments a frightful reality. Thus 'it is a fearful thing to fall into the hands of the living God', for 'mortal man, however inimical he may be, cannot carry his enmity beyond death, but the power of God is not confined to such narrow limits. We often escape from men, we cannot escape the judgment of God' (Calvin).

*V*32: **But call to remembrance the former days, in which, after ye were enlightened, ye endured a great conflict of sufferings;**

As with the earlier warning, so this is followed by words of encouragement [6:9f]. Here the author bids them recall a particular occasion, soon after their 'enlightenment', when their faith had emerged unscathed from a great contest of sufferings. Although this persecution was severe it appears from 12:4 that no Christian lives were lost, and this would rule out Jerusalem as the scene of their trial. W. Manson suggests that the Epistle was written to Jewish Christians in Rome shortly before Nero's bloodbath (AD 64), and that these verses (*vv* 32–34) refer to their experiences during AD 49 when the Emperor Claudius ordered all Jews to leave the city because, according to Suetonius, 'they were constantly indulging in riots at the instigation of Chrestus' [cf *Acts* 18:2]. 'If we assume that the name "Chrestus" here is a garbled form of Christus, the meaning will be that Messianic agitations breaking out among the Jews at Rome had drawn down upon them the unfavourable notice of the public authorities, the guardians of the peace, and Claudius acted accordingly . . . The most plausible explanation of the whole episode is that Christian propaganda had been introduced into the synagogues at Rome and had created considerable ferment' (W. Manson, *The Epistle to the Hebrews*, p. 41).

*V*33: **partly, being made a gazing-stock both by reproaches and afflictions; and partly, becoming partakers with them that were so used.**

This specifies the two ways in which the faith of the Hebrews had been severely tested soon after their conversion. Their own confession of Christ had brought them public reproaches and sufferings, and these afflictions were intensified by their voluntary association with fellow believers who were enduring the same persecution.

*V*34: **For ye both had compassion on them that were in bonds, and took joyfully the spoiling of your possessions, knowing that ye have for yourselves a better possession and an abiding one.**

Despite the personal risk involved, they did not shrink from visiting those of their brethren who were imprisoned for the sake of the gospel, and willingly ministered to their needs [*Matt* 25:36]. Moreover, they were enabled to meet the loss of their worldly goods with joyful fortitude because they knew that they had a better eternal inheritance. 'This will make a rich amends for all they can lose and suffer here. In heaven they shall have a better life, a better estate, better liberty, better society, better hearts, better work, every thing better' (Matthew Henry). [*Matt* 6:19–21; 1 *Pet* 1:4]

*V*35: **Cast not away therefore your boldness, which hath great recompense of reward.**

Since you showed such courage in those days, do not now cast away your confident confession which has 'great recompense of reward'. This is 'of a kind which no mercenary self-seeker would seek: holiness will be its own reward; self-devotion to Christ will be its own rich recompense' (Fausset). [*Gen* 15:1; *Matt* 5:12, 10:32]

*V*36: **For ye have need of patience, that, having done the will of God, ye may receive the promise.**

If they are to receive the promised salvation they have need of patience both to do and to bear the will of God. For it is only the recognition that the will of God includes the afflictions that accompany a profession of faith in Christ which enables the believer to sustain them [1 *Pet* 4:19]. 'The consideration of eternal life as the free effect of the grace of God and Christ, and as proposed in a gracious promise, is a thousand times more full of spiritual refreshment unto a believer, than if he should conceive of it or look upon it merely as a reward proposed unto our own doings or merits' (John Owen).

*V*37: **For yet a very little while,**
      He that cometh shall come, and shall not tarry.
*V*38: **But my righteous one shall live by faith:**
      And if he shrink back, my soul hath no pleasure in him.

The exhortation to patient endurance is now confirmed by a free quotation of *Hab* 2:3, 4 according to the Septuagint. In the original Hebrew the prophet is bidden to wait for the promised vision ('*it* will surely come'), whereas in the Greek version the advent of a person is awaited ('*he* will surely come'). This messianic interpretation is endorsed by the author, who also inverts the two parts of *Hab* 2:4

[v 38], so that '"my righteous one" becomes the subject of both parts of the verse' (F. F. Bruce).

For yet a very little while, The phrase may be a reminiscence of Is 26:20 Septuagint, but since the author's mind is so steeped in Scripture it is not necessary to assume that this is a conscious quotation. After having suffered so much they must not think the time has come to abandon their faith. Let them hold fast to their original confidence, and in a very little while they will receive the promise.

He that cometh shall come, and shall not tarry. For Christ shall soon appear and bestow the promised glory. 'He will most certainly come; his very name is still "the coming One". He has received that name because of his first coming but also because of his second coming' (Lenski). [cf Matt 11:3]

But my righteous one shall live by faith: Since the believer can only be described as God's 'righteous one' because he is justified by faith [cf Rom 1:17; Gal 3:11], he clearly cannot retain that standing before God unless he continues to believe. 'The apostle's purpose is to show that those who are reckoned just before God can only live by faith. The future tense of the word "live" shows the continuity of life' (Calvin).

And if he shrink back, my soul hath no pleasure in him. Yet *if* this same 'righteous' man were to shrink back, then God would take no pleasure in him, for only 'he that endureth to the end shall be saved' [Matt 10:22]. 'Christ hath no delights in dastards, turn-coats, run-a-ways, he will not employ them so far as to break a pitcher, or bear a torch, *Judges* 7:7' (Trapp).

*V*39: **But we are not of them that shrink back unto perdition; but of them that have faith unto the saving of the soul.**

Thus believers cannot escape from the necessity of choosing between these alternatives. They must realize that to renounce their interest in Christ is to 'shrink back unto perdition'. In that event their loss would be total and final. However, their past history convinces the writer that they will not prove to be reprobates, but that they are of that number who believe 'unto the saving of the soul'. And it is to inspire such perseverance that the illustrious faith of their ancestors is so splendidly recalled in the verses which now follow [11:1ff].

CHAPTER ELEVEN

To enforce the need of patient endurance, the author first explains the nature of faith, and then illustrates its achievements during the period of promise. His inspiring list of the great heroes of faith, who continued to trust in God through many trials, is roughly chronological and stretches from Abel to the Maccabean martyrs [vv 1–38]. This roll-call of faith serves to remind the readers of their greater privileges under the gospel. For though these noble men and women endured so much, they did not live to see their hope fulfilled in Christ: God having determined that the OldTestament saints should be perfected together with all New Testament believers [vv 39, 40].

*V*1: **Now faith is assurance of things hoped for, a conviction of things not seen.**

Now faith is confident assurance of the things we hope for (Arndt-Gingrich). Faith does not *give* 'substance' (av) to the things hoped for, but is rather the subjective assurance of their reality. It is solely because the objects of hope have an existence quite apart from faith that faith in them is not misplaced. It is this which distinguishes saving faith from the faith of the imagination, for only those who put their trust in the promises of God are delivered from embracing a miserable delusion. 'By *faith* we are sure of eternal things that they ARE; by *hope* we are confident that WE SHALL

HAVE them. Hope presupposes faith [*Rom* 8:25]' (Fausset).

a conviction of things not seen. Such faith is more than a bare assent to a set of theological propositions; it is a regulative principle of life [*Gal* 2:20]. Thus it was 'by faith' in what was unseen that the elders overcame all the obstacles which were presented to them by the eye of sense. As Moffatt observes, the writer is not giving an abstract definition of faith, but is describing it 'as an active conviction which moves and moulds human conduct. The happiest description of it is, "seeing Him who is invisible" [*v* 27]'.

*V*2: **For therein the elders had witness borne to them.**

Moreover it was 'in' (and not outside) the sphere and exercise of this faith that the fathers were approved of God, for without faith it is impossible to please him [*v* 6]. The statement thus prepares the readers for the great roll-call of faith which follows [*vv* 4–38]. They must realize that the achievements of the heroes they so much admire were all wrought 'by faith'. So if they now renounce their faith in Christ in order to return to Judaism, 'they do not desert *to* but *from* these men and these women and thereby place their names on that horrible list marked "Perdition" [10:39]' (Lenski).

*V*3: **By faith we understand that the worlds have been framed by the word of God so that what is seen hath not been made out of things which appear.**

Indeed it is faith alone which enables us to perceive that the universe was not made out of pre-existing materials but that it owes its existence to the creative word of God [*Gen* 1:3; *Ps* 33:6, 9]. 'Creation is here represented as a fact which we apprehend only by faith. By faith we understand (perceive, not comprehend) that the world was framed or fashioned by the word of God, that is, the word of God's power, the divine fiat, so that the things which are seen, the visible things of this world, were not made out of things which do appear, which are visible, and which are at least occasionally seen. According to this passage the world certainly was not made out of anything that is palpable to the senses' (L. Berkhof, *Systematic Theology*, pp. 133–134).

This verse therefore serves two important purposes: 1. It completes the author's description of faith by confirming that it is 'a conviction of things not seen' [*v* 1]; 2. It lays the essential foundation for the life of faith in all its manifestations. For without faith in God as the sovereign Creator of the world it is impossible to trust in his power to preserve and govern all things for the final good of his people [*Rom* 8:28; *Rev* 4:11].

*V*4: **By faith Abel offered unto God a more excellent sacrifice than Cain, through which he had witness borne to him that he was righteous, God bearing witness in respect of his gifts: and through it he being dead yet speaketh.**

The faith of Abel must not be artificially restricted to the spirit in which he offered his sacrifice, for it also includes his obedience to what must have been a divine appointment [*Rom* 10:17]. It was not by fancy, but by faith that he 'brought of the firstlings of his flock and of the fat thereof.' If Scripture does not provide us with an account of the institution of expiatory sacrifice, yet it can hardly be without significance that 'the very first recorded instance of acceptable worship in the family of Adam brings before us bleeding sacrifices, and seals them with the divine approbation. They appear in the first act of worship, *Gen* 4:3, 4. They are emphatically approved by God as soon as they appear' (A. A. Hodge, *The Atonement*, p. 124). The worship of Cain was not accepted, because he wilfully ignored the consequences of the fall. His gift of 'the fruit of the ground' merely acknowledged God as the creator and sustainer of life, whereas saving faith is pre-eminently faith in the promised redemption [*Gen* 3:15].

God must have visibly signified his acceptance of Abel's offering for Cain was displeased by it. It is likely that he sent fire from heaven to consume the sacrifice [*Gen* 15:7; *Lev* 9:24; *Judges* 6:21; 1 *Kings* 18:38; 2 *Chron* 7:1]. 'Whomsoever God accepts or respects, he testifieth him to be righteous; that is, to be justified, and freely accepted with him. This Abel was by faith antecedently unto his offering. He was not made righteous, he was not justified by his sacrifice; but therein he showed his faith by his works: and God by acceptance of his works of obedience justified him, as Abraham was justified by works; namely, declaratively; he declared him so to be' (John Owen).

In adducing the example the Abel the author evidently has in mind its particular bearing upon those who were being persecuted for their faith [12:4], for as he later shows, the blood of faith's *first* martyr still cries to God for vindication [12:24; cf *Gen* 4:10; *Rev* 6:9–11]. 'Thus, Abel is not only a type of the persecution and suffering of the godly, but gives a pledge of the certain vengeance which God will take in due time upon their oppressors' (A. W. Pink). [*Luke* 18:7, 8]

V5: **By faith Enoch was translated that he should not see death; and he was not found, because God translated him: for he hath had witness borne to him that before his translation he had been well-pleasing unto God:**

Enoch, like Elijah after him [2 *Kings* 2:11], did not taste death, for God took him directly to heaven. This immediate glorification of the body is also to be shared by those who are alive at Christ's coming [1 *Cor* 15:51, 52; 1 *Thess* 4:16, 17]. 'This verse does not teach that Enoch had faith to be translated. God translated him because he lived a life in which He was pleased. It was by faith that he lived that life. The Mosaic commentary on his life is in the words "Enoch walked with God" [*Gen* 5:22]' (K. Wuest).

Since Enoch was spiritually 'translated' [*Col* 1:13] long before his physical removal from the earth, it follows that those who wish to join God in heaven must first give evidence on earth of a similar transformation of heart and life [*Rom* 12:2]. 'He changed his place, but not his company, for he still walked with God, as in earth, so in heaven' (Trapp). The second part of the verse means: Enoch pleased God *prior* to his translation and this fact is permanently recorded in the witness borne to him by the Scripture *after* his translation.

*V*6: **and without faith it is impossible to be well-pleasing unto him; for he that cometh to God must believe that he is, and that he is a rewarder of them that seek after him.**

Before he goes on to speak of Noah, the author here pauses to apply the lesson that the Hebrews must learn from the example of Enoch. Since *Gen* 5:22–24 affirms that Enoch was well-pleasing to God, he must have been a man of faith, for without faith it is impossible to please him at all. 'Where God hath put an impossibility upon any thing, it is in vain for men to attempt it. From the days of Cain multitudes have been designing to please God without faith, – all in vain; like them that would have built a tower whose top should reach to heaven' (John Owen).

And this means that the man who draws near to God must believe that he is, and that he is a rewarder of them that seek after him. The first point involves far more than a notional assent to the existence of a 'First Cause' or 'Supreme Being'; it is to believe in the self-existent living God as he has been pleased to reveal himself in his works, in his Word, and in his Son [1:2]. Secondly, the man of faith will approach God with the conviction that he will graciously receive and reward him [*Gen* 15:1; *Jer* 29:13]. 'So that Enoch's faith, and the faith of every one who approaches God, verifies the description of *v* 1: the unseen must be treated as sufficiently demonstrated, and the hoped-for reward must be considered substantial' (Marcus Dods).

*V*7: **By faith Noah, being warned of God concerning things not seen as yet, moved with godly fear, prepared an ark to the saving of his house; through which he condemned the world, and became heir of the righteousness which is according to faith.**

Noah received the warning of the impending deluge with implicit faith despite every appearance to the contrary, and, filled with reverential awe, he built an ark for the saving of his family. During the 120 years of God's longsuffering the faithful witness of Noah as 'a preacher of righteousness' amounted to a divine condemnation of the universal unbelief which greeted his unwelcome message. Thus Noah's righteous conduct attested the reality of his justification, for his interest in 'the righteousness which is according to faith' (i.e. *by the rule of, on a principle of faith*, cf *Rom* 4:13, 9:30, 10:6) was proved by his unswerving fidelity to this exacting commission [*Gen* 6:9f; 2 *Pet* 2:5]. 'The example is the more instructive, as it naturally, and almost necessarily, brings before the mind the fearfully destructive efficiency of unbelief. The world that perished had materially the same message delivered to them as that which Noah received. Had they repented, there is no reason to doubt that the fearful infliction would not have taken place. Noah believed, and feared, and obeyed, and was saved. They disbelieved, and mocked, and were disobedient, and perished' (John Brown).

*V*8: **By faith Abraham, when he was called, obeyed to go out unto a place which he was to receive for an inheritance; and he went out, not knowing whither he went.**

This verse begins the section in which the faith of the patriarchs is reviewed [*vv* 8–22]. Abraham was by nature no different from any other child of Adam, for until he was called by the Lord he lived with his family in the heathen city of Ur where they 'served other gods' [*Josh* 24:2]. God had no plans for the conversion of that city, but it was his will to call one man out of it. Abraham at once obeyed the divine demand to renounce the past, leaving home for an unspecified destination, thus acknowledging that he had been effectually called by the grace of God [*Gen* 12:1f]. This call is distinguished from all other plausible pretences by the unquestioning obedience which it secures. 'Obedience is faith's daughter. Faith hath not only to do with the grace of God, but with the duty of the creature' (Thomas Manton).

to go out unto a place which he was to receive for an inheritance; It is clear from *v* 10 that Abraham looked for a better inheritance than the land of promise in which he lived as a stranger. Indeed the author is at pains to point out that the pilgrim life of the patriarchs proved that they hoped for far more than the possession of an earthly inheritance, and this was because their faith had grasped the spiritual nature of the promise [*vv* 13–16].

and he went out, not knowing whither he went. If Abraham knew not whither he went, yet he knew who had called him, and that was enough. 'Abraham winked, as it were, and put his hand into God's, to be led whithersoever he pleased' (Trapp). In the same way the readers are to abandon the visible shadows of Judaism in favour of the invisible substance of Christianity [2 *Cor* 4:18]. 'Nothing but the faith of the gospel can induce a man to abandon the world and commence a pilgrimage towards heaven. And wherever there is the faith of the gospel, there will be the commencement and prosecution of such a pilgrimage. If Abraham had continued in Mesopotamia, or stopped short of Canaan, it would have been a proof that he did not believe the divine testimony; and whatever men may profess, if they continue to love the world, and become "weary in well-doing," it is clear evidence that they have not believed the gospel' (John Brown). [2 *Tim* 4:10]

*V*9: **By faith he became a sojourner in the land of promise, as in a land not his own, dwelling in tents, with Isaac and Jacob, the heirs with him of the same promise:**

Moreover faith enabled Abraham, as it did Isaac and Jacob after him, to live as self-confessed aliens in the land of promise, dwelling in tents, without so much as a square foot to call their own, except for the purchase of a burial place for Sarah [*Gen* 23; *Acts* 7:5]. 'The tent-life of the patriarchs demonstrated their pilgrim character: it made manifest their contentment to live upon the *surface* of the earth, for a tent has no foundation, and can be pitched or struck at short notice. They were sojourners here and just passing through this wilderness-scene without striking their roots into it' (A. W. Pink). He whose heart is fixed upon things above holds but loosely to the things of earth [*Col* 3:1, 2]. 'A little in the world will content a Christian for his passage, but all the world, and ten thousand times more, will not content a Christian for his portion' (Jeremiah Burroughs, *The Rare Jewel of Christian Contentment*, p. 43). [13:5; *Phil* 4:11; 1 *Tim* 6:6, 8]

*V*10: **for he looked for the city which hath the foundations, whose builder and maker is God.**

Abraham was content with his earthly lot because he looked for that city with unshakeable foundations [12:28] 'whose architect and maker is God' (ASV margin). 'There is *an instinct of immortality* in saintship. He who lives to God *knows* that he must live for ever (Matt. 22:32)' (Vaughan). The word 'city' not only suggests the idea of permanence, but also brings to mind an ordered society under the divine government. 'The object of his desire was social and not personal only' (Westcott).

*V*II: **By faith even Sarah herself received power to conceive seed when she was past age, since she counted him faithful who had promised:**

This takes note of Sarah's faith, though Abraham remains the subject of the sentence as in *v* 9: **By faith he also, together with Sarah, received power to beget a child** (H. H. Esser, *NIDNTT*, Vol. I p. 378). 'At first she laughed, through unbelief, at the unlikelihood; but afterward she bethought herself, and believed. This latter is recorded, the former pardoned. So *Gen* 18:12, 'Sarah laughed within herself, saying, After I have waxen old shall I have pleasure, my lord being old also?' Here was never a good word but one, viz. that she called her husband lord, and this is recorded to her eternal commendation, 1 *Pet* 3:6. Isaac then was not a child of nature, but of the mere promise; so are all our graces. We bring forth good things, as Sarah's dead womb brought forth a child' (Trapp).

*V*12: **wherefore also there sprang of one, and him as good as dead, so many as the stars of heaven in multitude, and as the sand, which is by the sea-shore, innumerable.**

As was shown in the previous verse, Sarah shared her husband's faith in the divine promise, and in fact her belief in the revelation that she would bear a son was a condition for the fruitfulness of Abraham's faith. 'If the Jews are now proud of their origin, they must look to its cause. Whatever they are is to be attributed to the faith of Abraham and Sarah. It follows from this that they cannot hold or defend the position which they have atttained except on the basis of faith' (Calvin). [*Gen* 15:5, 17:15–22, 22:17; *Is* 51:1, 2; *Rom* 4:16–21]

*V*13: **These all died in faith, not having received the promises, but having seen them and greeted them from**

**afar, and having confessed that they were strangers
and pilgrims on the earth.**

These all died in faith, The verses which follow [*vv* 13–16]
cannot apply to the antediluvians mentioned by the author
for they were not pilgrims in a strange land, and of course
Enoch did not die! They rather point the lesson to be learned
from the eminent example set by the founders of Israel
[*vv* 8–12]. This verse conveys something more than an objective account of their obedience; it 'gives an internal
picture of their mind and how they felt themselves to be,
a consciousness which they preserved even up to death'
(A. B. Davidson).

not having received the promises, Since God was pleased
on numerous occasions to confirm and expand the original
promise made to Abraham, the plural is used here. Thus
the patriarchs believed the promises, which were centred in
the Messiah through whom all the nations of the earth were
to be blessed, yet they all died without having seen their
fulfilment [*vv* 39, 40]. If then they lived and died triumphantly
on bare promises, how dare those who have seen their
fulfilment falter in their allegiance to Christ?

but having seen them and greeted them from afar,
'They were like pilgrims to the Holy City who see its towers
and spires on the horizon, ecstatically point to the vision, and
shout their acclaim. This is all they had during their earthly
lives' (Lenski). [*John* 8:56]

**and having confessed that they were strangers and pil-
grims on the earth.** As the reality of their heavenly calling
made evident their renunciation of the world, they inevitably
attracted the *hostility* which was accorded to 'strangers' in
the ancient world, while as 'pilgrims' or 'sojourners' they
willingly bore the *stigma* of having no rights of residence
in an alien land [cf *Eph* 2:12ff; *Phil* 3:20].

*V*14: **For they that say such things make it manifest that they are seeking after a country of their own.**

In confessing themselves to be pilgrims on earth they declared that their true homeland was in heaven. 'Whosoever professes he has a Father in heaven, confesses himself a stranger on earth; hence there is in the heart an ardent longing, like that of a child among strangers, in want and grief, far from his *fatherland*' (Luther).

*V*15: **And if indeed they had been mindful of that country from which they went out, they would have had opportunity to return.**

Indeed if their thoughts had been fixed upon the country they had left then there was nothing to stop their return to it. Hence their exile was entirely voluntary. In the same way the readers had ample opportunity to end their pilgrimage of faith and return to the attractions of Judaism. But those who are truly called of God do not revert to the old life, not for lack of opportunity, but because they no longer desire it; whereas Demas returned to this present world for no other reason than that he still loved it! [2 *Tim* 4:10]

*V*16: **But now they desire a better country, that is, a heavenly: wherefore God is not ashamed of them, to be called their God; for he hath prepared for them a city.**

The patriarchs had this sense of exile because their hearts were set on a better country and firmer settlement than could be found anywhere, but in heaven. By this expectation they gave God the credit for meaning more by his promises than the *letter* indicated, for they had respect to their *spirit* rather than the thing promised. Hence God is not ashamed to be called their God, and this is proved by the fact that he has prepared for them a city to justify the expectations which they had based upon his power and goodness. The patriarchs showed that they understood that God, in giving these promises, became their God; therefore God was not ashamed of them, and this showed itself especially in his naming himself 'the God of Abraham, Isaac and Jacob' [*Exod* 3:15]. (so Marcus Dods)

*V*17: **By faith Abraham, being tried, offered up Isaac: yea, he that had gladly received the promises was offering up his only begotten son;**
*V*18: **even he to whom it was said, In Isaac shall thy seed be called:**
*V*19: **accounting that God is able to raise up, even from the dead; from whence he did also in a figure receive him back.**

As there could be no fulfilment of the divine promise without Isaac, the command to sacrifice his only son was the supreme test of Abraham's faith in God [*Gen* 21:12, 22:1–18]. God normally tries the faith of his people by requiring their continued trust in his word despite the occasional *apparent* contradictions of his providential dealings with them. But Abraham was subjected to a far more severe test, because the command to slay Isaac was in *direct* contradiction to the promise that 'In Isaac shall thy seed be called'.

But Abraham refused to let his obedience to the command cancel his trust in the promise, for he reckoned that God was well able to raise up his son even from the dead [*Gen* 22:5]. And it was because Abraham was actually in the process of offering up Isaac when he was stopped, that the receiving back of his son was virtually a resurrection from the dead. For though 'Isaac did not in fact rise from the dead, yet it seemed to be a kind of resurrection when he was snatched back suddenly and miraculously by the unexpected grace of God' (Calvin).

*V*20: **By faith Isaac blessed Jacob and Esau, even concerning things to come.**

By faith Isaac believed the revelation which God made to him concerning the respective destinies of Jacob and Esau. And it was because he was fully conscious of the inspiration under which he had spoken that he made no attempt to revoke the blessing after the discovery of Jacob's deceit [Gen 27:33]. Instead he bowed to the divine decree even though it set aside the law of primogeniture and overruled his own inclinations [Rom 9:10–13].

The Hebrew Christians also had received a revelation of things to come to which they must either give their unhesitating assent or else resign themselves to sharing Esau's bitter lot [12:16, 17].

V21: **By faith Jacob, when he was dying, blessed each of the sons of Joseph; and worshipped, leaning upon the top of his staff.**

It was faith which enabled Jacob, when he lay dying in Egypt, to predict the future inheritance of Ephraim and Manasseh in Canaan [Gen 48:1f]. The inference here is that those who do not lay hold of the promised blessings in faith cannot be the true descendants of the one who did.

and worshipped, leaning upon the top of his staff. This incident took place before the patriarchal benediction mentioned in the first part of the verse [Gen 47:31]. The difference between the Septuagint, 'upon the top of his staff,' and the Hebrew, 'upon the bed's head,' is only a matter of punctuation. The Septuagint reads the unpointed Hebrew word M-TT-H as MATTEH, *staff*, whereas it is pointed in the Massoretic text as MITTAH, *bed*. In this instance it seems likely that the former is the more accurate reading, and it certainly makes better sense. As death drew near, Jacob made Joseph swear that he would not leave his body in Egypt but that it would be taken to Canaan for burial there, and then he worshipped God, supporting his now feeble frame upon his staff, which was the symbol of his pilgrim state [*Gen* 32:10]. Thus the fact that Jacob arranged to take possession of Canaan, 'as it were, by his dead body, was a very strong expression of his full persuasion that in due time his posterity should, according to the divine promise, possess it as an inheritance' (John Brown).

*V*22: **By faith Joseph, when his end was nigh, made mention of the departure of the children of Israel; and gave commandment concerning his bones.**

At the end of his long life Joseph predicted the exodus of the children of Israel from Egypt, saying, 'God will surely visit you' [*Gen* 50:24, 25]. As one who was second only to Pharaoh himself, his body might well have been laid to rest in some grand Egyptian tomb, but he entertained a far higher hope than this. For he publicly expressed his faith in the promised salvation by commanding that his bones should 'join in the exodus from Egypt and be buried in Canaan. 'To take an example from hence of digging men's bones out of their graves, of enshrining and placing them on altars, of carrying them up and down in procession, of adoring them with all signs of religious veneration, applying them unto miraculous operations, in curing diseases, casting out of devils, and the like, is fond [foolish] and ridiculous' (John Owen).

*V*23: **By faith Moses, when he was born, was hid three months by his parents, because they saw he was a goodly child; and they were not afraid of the king's command-ment.**

Five examples of faith from the life of Israel's greatest leader, Moses, are next instanced, the first of which recalls the faith of his parents [*vv* 23–29]. When Amram and Jochebed saw the beauty of Moses they resolved to defy the barbarous mandate which ordered the death of every son born of Heb-rew parents, and they hid him in the house for three months, not fearing Pharaoh's impious decree [*Exod* 2:2; *Acts* 7:19]. They evidently believed the beauty of their child to be a special token of the divine favour which marked him out for a high destiny [cf *Acts* 7:20 ASV margin, 'Moses . . . was fair unto God']. We are not told whether they received a more specific revelation of God's will concerning the child, but in any case 'some appreciation of the divine purpose to be fulfilled through Moses is implied in the author's ascription of faith to Amram and Jochebed' (F. F. Bruce).

*V*24: **By faith Moses, when he was grown up, refused to be called the son of Pharaoh's daughter;**
*V*25: **choosing rather to share ill treatment with the people of God, than to enjoy the pleasures of sin for a season;**

When Moses was forty years old he renounced the position he enjoyed in Egypt as the adopted son of Pharaoh's daughter in order to share the reproach of the people of God [*Exod* 2:11, 12; *Acts* 7:23, 24]. This was not the act of a pioneer revolutionary made in the interests of any earthly Utopia. It was not because he was of the same race that Moses chose to share the lot of a persecuted people, but because he knew them to be 'the people of God'. 'The faith of Moses enabled him to estimate aright the objects before him, and to forecast the future of the People of God, and oppose it to the temporary glory of sin. "Sin" in his case would have been apostasy, and there lies a delicate appeal to the Hebrews in his example' (A. B. Davidson).

the pleasures of sin 'It is a common thing for a scripture to speak of a certain thing as if it were, and to say that it is, when it is only supposed to be so by others. For example, 'There be gods many, and lords many' [1 *Cor* 8:5]; not that there really were any such gods, but that by others they were reckoned so to be. Similarly in this text, he speaks according to the manner of men concerning the pleasures of sin, as they are reputed . . . It is false pleasure, and what truer misery is there than false joy? It is like the pleasure of the man who receives much money, but it is all counterfeit, or the pleasure of the man who dreams of a feast and awakes so hungry and vexed that he could eat his dream. For this reason sin should be doubly hated, because it is ugly and false, because it defiles and mocks us' (Ralph Venning, *The Plague of Plagues*, pp. 208–210).

V26: accounting the reproach of Christ greater riches than the treasures of Egypt: for he looked unto the recompense of reward.

Geerhardus Vos points out that the phrase 'the reproach of Christ' is explained by the exhortation, 'Let us therefore go forth unto him without the camp, bearing his reproach' [13:13]. 'This reproach is thus seen to be a reproach which Christ Himself first bore and which we now bear together with Him. So we must similarly interpret the reproach of Christ borne by Moses. This does not imply that Moses had a prophetic knowledge of the sufferings of the future Messiah, but rather that the reproach which Moses bore was objectively identical with the reproach suffered by Christ and His people throughout the ages. This implies, therefore, that back of all the reproaches and sufferings which God's people have endured, stood Christ. How this appeared to Moses' own subjective consciousness is told us in 11:25, "choosing rather to share ill treatment with the people of God..."'

for he looked unto the recompense of reward. The fleeting treasures of Egypt could not capture Moses' affections for he looked forward to an eternal inheritance [*v* 6]. 'Let the things of this world be increased and multiplied into the greatest measures and degrees imaginable, it alters not their kind. – They are temporary, fading, and perishing still; such as will stand men in no stead on their greatest occasions, nor with respect unto eternity' (John Owen).

*V*27: **By faith he forsook Egypt, not fearing the wrath of the king: for he endured, as seeing him who is invisible.**

The strange attempt to reconcile this verse with Moses' fearful flight to Midian should be abandoned [*Exod* 2:14, 15]. It must refer to the events associated with the exodus which is here ascribed to the faith of Moses because it was accomplished under his inspired leadership. 'Not fearing the wrath of the king' describes his fearless demeanour before Pharaoh as he repeatedly demanded the release of God's people [*Exod* 10:28, 29]. By 'seeing him who is invisible' Moses withstood the wrath of this earthly potentate, and was able to lead the children of Israel out of Egypt without fear of what might be done to prevent their escape.

*V*28: **By faith he kept the passover, and the sprinkling of the blood, that the destroyer of the firstborn should not touch them.**

Moses 'instituted the passover' (ASV margin) for no other reason than that God had commanded it. He instructed the people to offer the appointed sacrifice and to sprinkle their door posts with the blood, for he was fully persuaded that this unusual measure would protect them from the destroyer as he passed through the land in terrible judgment [*Exod* 12].

'That which God would for ever instruct the church in by this ordinance is, that unless we are sprinkled with the blood of Christ, our paschal Lamb, no other privilege can secure us from eternal destruction. – Though a man had been really an Israelite and had with others made himself ready that night for a departure, which was a high profession of faith, yet if the lintel and posts of his door had not been sprinkled with blood, he would have been destroyed. And on the other hand, where there is this sprinkling of blood, be the danger never so great or so near, there shall be certain deliverance. "The blood of sprinkling speaks better things than the blood of Abel'" (John Owen). [*John* 1:29; 1 *Cor* 5:7]

*V*29: **By faith they passed through the Red sea as by dry land: which the Egyptians assaying to do were swallowed up.**

As John Owen notes, 'the whole is denominated from the better part,' for the vast majority of those who passed safely through the Red Sea later perished miserably in the wilderness because of their unbelief [3:7–19; *Exod* 14:11; 1 *Cor* 10:5]. But on this occasion the temporal deliverance of the many was effected by the saving faith of the few: e.g. Moses, Aaron, Caleb, and Joshua [*Rom* 9:6].

which the Egyptians assaying to do were swallowed up.
'*Rash presumption* mistaken by many for *faith*: with similar presumption many rush into eternity. The same thing done by the believer and by the unbeliever is not the same thing. What was *faith* in Israel was *presumption* in the Egyptians' (Fausset).

*V*30: **By faith the walls of Jericho fell down, after they had been compassed about for seven days.**

The next example of faith which is celebrated by the author is separated from the exodus by an interval of forty years. This period is passed over in silence because he regards the wanderings in the wilderness as the years of unbelief. A signal instance of the power of united faith is provided by the fall of Jericho, for after Joshua and the children of Israel had marched silently round this apparently impregnable citadel for seven days its walls at last collapsed before their triumphant shout of faith. The Hebrews are called to a similar exercise of faith in the power of God to conquer all the bastions of unbelief [*Josh* 6; *Zech* 4:6–7; 2 *Cor* 10:3–5].

*V*31: **By faith Rahab the harlot perished not with them that were disobedient, having received the spies with peace.**

No doubt the surprising inclusion of Rahab in the roll of those whose faith is specially praised is an implied rebuke to the readers [*Josh* 2]. For if an Amorite harlot believed the reports she had heard of the God of Israel so that she 'perished not with them that were disobedient', then how can the children of the covenant renounce their interest in the promised Messiah? Calvin says that she is only described as 'the harlot' in order to magnify the grace of God in reclaiming her from such a disgraceful past, for it is certain that 'her faith is the evidence of her repentance'. [*Josh* 6:25; *James* 2:25] Indeed she later married a prince of Judah, and shares with 'Ruth the Moabitess' an honoured place in the genealogy of the Saviour himself [*Matt* 1:5].

*V*32: **And what shall I more say? for the time will fail me if I tell of Gideon, Barak, Samson, Jephthah; of David and Samuel and the prophets:**

Although the list is far from exhausted, lack of time forces the author rapidly to sum up the achievements [*vv* 32–34] and the sufferings of faith [*vv* 35–38] in a brilliant final paragraph. The order remains roughly chronological, for apart from David, all those named here belong to the period of the Judges, while some of the later descriptions clearly refer to the courageous endurance of the Maccabean martyrs. By this rhetorical device the readers are faced with a long line of witnesses who remained faithful to their calling. Will they now waver in theirs?

*V*33: **who through faith subdued kingdoms, wrought righteousness, obtained promises, stopped the mouths of lions,**

*V*34: **quenched the power of fire, escaped the edge of the sword, from weakness were made strong, waxed mighty in war, turned to flight armies of aliens.**

A powerful impression is produced by the cumulative effect of this swift inventory of faith's exploits. With all the skill of an orator, the writer, in nine terse clauses delivered in 'sledge-hammer style' (Robertson), invites them to 'See what faith has wrought!' Some of the items are readily identified; others have a more general reference.

who through faith subdued kingdoms, Gideon conquered the Midianites [*Judges* 7]; Barak the Canaanites [*Judges* 4]; Samson the Philistines [*Judges* 14f]; Jephthah the Ammonites [*Judges* 11]; and David the Philistines [2 *Sam* 5:17], the Moabites [2 *Sam* 8:2], and the Ammonites [2 *Sam* 10:12]. That all those victories were achieved with weaker forces than those of their enemies demonstrates that faith is a mighty weapon! [cf 1 *Sam* 14:6].

wrought righteousness, This probably refers to the righteous rule exercised by those mentioned in the previous verse [cf 2 *Sam* 8:15]. 'Conquerors used their success for the furtherance of right. Righteousness was shown to be the solid foundation of enduring power: *Is* 9:7, 54:14; 1 *Kings* 10:9' (Westcott).

obtained promises, The Old Testament saints lived long enough to see many promises fulfilled, though they died without having seen the fulfilment of the Messianic promises [cf *vv* 13, 39].

stopped the mouths of lions, In the next three clauses personal deliverance is in view. The first may be referred to the youthful exploits of Samson and David [*Judges* 14:5, 6; 1 *Sam* 17:35], and to Daniel's courage in his old age [*Dan* 6:22].

quenched the power of fire, Here Shadrach, Meshach, and Abed-nego at once spring to mind [*Dan* 3:12ff]. 'It was not only the flame, but the very nature of the fire, which in the power of faith they quenched and overcame, when they walked in "the midst of the furnace"' (Delitzsch).

escaped the edge of the sword, Either in battle, or when pursued by enemies, as David escaped from Saul [1 *Sam* 18:11], and Elijah from Jezebel [1 *Kings* 19:3].

from weakness were made strong, The last three clauses show how God's strength was received through faith. Although the main reference here is probably to Samson [*Judges* 16:28], Hezekiah's recovery from sickness may not be ruled out [2 *Kings* 20:1–7].

waxed mighty in war, A possible reminiscence of Barak's annihilation of Sisera's host [*Judges* 4:16], though all Israel's notable victories were the fruit of faith in the divine promise [cf 2 *Chron* 14:9–12; 20:14–25].

turned to flight armies of aliens. In 'aliens' we have 'a comprehensive word for the enemies of Israel all along the sacred history, but it certainly includes the Maccabean struggle, and so prepares for the distinct reference to that later period in the verses which follow' (Vaughan).

*V*35: **women received their dead by a resurrection: and others were tortured, not accepting their deliverance; that they might obtain a better resurrection:**

The author now begins a harrowing account of what faith can suffer. 'There was never any greater instance of the degeneracy of human nature unto the image and likeness of the devil than this, that so many of them have been found, and that in high places of power, emperors, kings, judges, and priests, who were not satisfied to take away the lives of the true worshippers of God by the sword, or by such other ways as they slew the worst of malefactors, but invented all kinds of hellish tortures whereby to destroy them' (John Owen). In this verse an extreme contrast is drawn between the women who were delivered from the suffering of bereavement by a resurrection which restored their children to an earthly life [1 *Kings* 17:17–24; 2 *Kings* 4:18–37], and the refusal of the Maccabean martyrs to recant under the most fiendish tortures because they looked for 'a better resurrection' than a mere respite from earthly suffering [2 *Macc* 7:9, 11, 14; 2 *Cor* 4:17, 18].

*V*36: **and others had trial of mockings and scourgings, yea, moreover of bonds and imprisonment:**
*V*37: **they were stoned, they were sawn asunder, they were tempted, they were slain with the sword: they went about in sheepskins, in goatskins; being destitute, afflicted, ill-treated**

Others whose sufferings fell short of martyrdom, nevertheless endured cruel mockery, scourging, bonds, and imprisonment [e.g. 1 *Kings* 22:24–27; *Jer* 20:2, 37:15], while some were stoned, sawn asunder, or slain with the sword. In view of the context many regard the words 'were tempted' as an incongruous insertion, but A. B. Davidson points out that the MS. authority favours this reading and that 'the reference must be to cruel tortures practised on men to procure apostasy'. According to tradition Jeremiah was stoned to death in Egypt, and Isaiah was sawn asunder during Manasseh's evil reign (for biblical examples, see 2 *Chron* 24:20–22; *Jer* 26:23). The same fidelity to God forced others to wander about like wild animals, destitute of even the common necessities of life.

*V*38: **(of whom the world was not worthy), wandering in deserts and mountains and caves, and the holes of the earth.**

The author's parenthetic judgment is well expounded by Trapp: 'They were fitter to be set as stars in heaven, and be before the Lord in his glory. The world was not worthy of their presence, and yet they were not thought worthy to live in the world.' On 'caves' Fausset remarks, 'Palestine, from its hilly character, abounds in fissures and caves, affording shelter to the persecuted, as the fifty hid by Obadiah and Elijah [1 *Kings* 18:4, 13, 19:8, 13]; Mattathias and his sons [1 *Macc* 2:28, 29]; Judas Maccabeus [2 *Macc* 5:27].'

*V*39: **And these all, having had witness borne to them through their faith, received not the promise,
40: God having provided some better things concerning us, that apart from us they should not be made perfect.**

Even though all these heroes obtained a good report through faith, they did not receive the fulfilment of the promise during their life on earth. For 'God had something better in view for us, (and so purposed) that they should not attain the Perfection apart from us' (W. Manson's translation). Or as Moffatt explains it: 'God in his good providence reserved the messianic *perfection* of Jesus Christ until we could share it'. Thus the Old Testament saints could not reach 'perfection' without us because the fulfilment of that promise awaited our day! For though they have already attained the bliss that belongs to 'the spirits of just men made perfect' [12:23], the final consummation of their hope still awaits the end of the age [9:28], when all the people of God shall be glorified together. 'If those on whom the great light of grace had not yet shone showed such patience in bearing their ills, what effect ought the full light of the gospel to have on us? A tiny spark of light led them to heaven, but now that the sun of righteousness shines on us what excuse shall we offer if we still hold to the earth?' (Calvin).

CHAPTER TWELVE

Since such a noble succession of witnesses have gone before them, the Hebrews are urged to discard every weight and to run with patience the race that is set before them, looking unto Jesus the pioneer and perfecter of faith, who endured the cross for the sake of the joy that was set before him and is now seated at the right hand of God [vv 1, 2]. When they consider what he suffered for them, they have no cause to become faint-hearted, especially if they remember that God's fatherly chastisements prove their sonship and also serve to make them partakers of his holiness [vv 3–10]. Although no chastening is enjoyable at the time, it afterwards yields the fruit of righteousness in those who are exercised by it. Therefore they must brace themselves for the conflict, and pursue peace with all men and the sanctification without which no man shall see the Lord; looking carefully lest any man should despise his spiritual birthright after the evil example of Esau who found no place of repentance, though he sought it diligently with tears [vv 11–17]. In Christ they are not confronted with the terrible portents of a vanished legal order, for they have not come to Mount Sinai but to the heavenly realm of Mount Zion, in which the redeemed rejoice before God through the merits of the Mediator whose blood speaks better than that of Abel [vv 18–24]. If they refuse to hear God who now speaks to them from heaven in the Person of his Son, they will incur a far more dreadful judgment than that which befell the despisers of the law. As therefore we receive through Christ a kingdom which cannot be shaken, let us serve God with godly fear, remembering that he is a consuming fire [vv 25–29].

*V*1: **Therefore let us also, seeing we are compassed about with so great a cloud of witnesses, lay aside every weight, and the sin which doth so easily beset us, and let us run with patience the race that is set before us,**

Therefore let us also, The author again graciously identifies himself with his disheartened readers [10:39], in order to encourage them to exercise the same faith by which their distinguished 'forerunners' were approved of God [11:4-40].

seeing we are compassed about with so great a cloud of witnesses, This does not mean that this host of 'witnesses' are the heavenly spectators of what takes place in the earthly arena, for as used here the word almost has the sense of 'martyr' [cf *Acts* 22:20; *Rev* 2:13, 17:6]. As Lenski points out, it is unbiblical to suggest that the spirits of the departed are still hovering about us to watch our progress. 'These saints are not "witnesses" that see our faith and testify about us; God does not ask them to testify about us. They are witnesses whose life, works, sufferings, death attest their own faith, and testify to us through the pages of Holy Writ and in other history that they were true men of faith indeed'.

lay aside every weight, As the athlete disciplines himself to discard everything that would impede his progress in the contest for which he has entered, so also every weight must be laid aside in the Christian race. An immoderate use of that which is not in itself sinful can become a great hindrance to the Christian. 'The Christian runner must rid himself even of innocent things which might retard him. And all that does not help, hinders. It is by running he learns what these things are. So long as he stands he does not feel that they are burdensome and hampering' (Marcus Dods). [cf *Phil* 3:8-14]

[172]

and the sin which doth closely cling to us, (ASV margin)
The figure compares sin to a loose garment entangling the
limbs of the runner, which thus reduces his speed and retards
him in his course. The reference is not to some sin in particular,
but to sin itself. As Vaughan remarks, The AV rendering 'the
sin which doth so easily beset us' catches 'the point of the
expression admirably until it is perverted into *the besetting sin*
as something different from *the whole body of sin*'. Those
who would be reckoned as serious competitors in this race
must therefore strip off the clinging garment of sin!

and let us run with patience the race that is set before us,
After the negative preparation comes the positive demand for
persistent progress. 'Patience' is not passive forbearance,
but 'patient endurance'. It is the lack of stamina that distinguishes the would-be contestant from the successful athlete.
In the Christian race, which is not a short sprint but a long-
distance contest, there are no prizes for those who do not
persevere to the end of the course [contrast *Acts* 20:24; 2 *Tim*
4:7, 8].

*V*2: **looking unto Jesus the author and perfecter of our
faith, who for the joy that was set before him endured
the cross, despising shame, and hath sat down at the
right hand of the throne of God.**

looking unto Jesus The author now reveals the great secret
of Christian perseverance. The strength to run this race is
only imparted when our gaze is constantly fixed upon the
great object of faith. 'Nor shall we endure any longer than
whilst the eye of our faith is fixed on him. From him alone
do we derive our refreshments in all our trials' (John Owen).

the pioneer and perfecter of faith, This glory belongs
uniquely to Jesus because: 1. As the *founder* of faith he alone
blazed the trail of salvation [2:10]; 2. As the *example* of faith

he alone brought faith to its perfection. 'Christ in the days of his flesh trod undeviatingly the path of faith, and as the Perfecter has brought it to a perfect end in his own person. Thus he is the leader of all others who tread that path' (W. E. Vine).

who for the joy that was set before him endured the cross, despising shame, This indicates the nature of Christ's example. As in *v* 16, the preposition *anti* means 'in exchange for': just as Esau sold his birthright for the price of a single meal, so in order to gain the joy that was set before him Jesus paid the price of the 'cross' (the word occurs only here in the Epistle), despising its shame. The joy envisaged was not a selfish joy; it was the joy to be achieved through that redemption which would accomplish the salvation of all his people [*Is* 53:11].

and hath sat down at the right hand of the throne of God. In drawing attention to the contrast between he 'endured' and 'hath sat down,' Westcott comments: 'The fact of suffering is wholly past but the issue of it abides for evermore'. Thus faith recognizes 'this Jesus' as the One whom God has made 'both Lord and Christ' [*Acts* 2:36]. He who once suffered on earth now rules from heaven [*Matt* 28:18]. The Hebrews must believe this however much present circumstances may appear to contradict it [12:3f]. And so must we!

*V*3: **For consider him that hath endured such gainsaying of sinners against himself, that ye wax not weary, fainting in your souls.**

'For' introduces the reason for fixing their gaze upon Jesus; to consider what he had to endure will show how light their sufferings are by comparison. Let them reflect upon what it meant for the *sinless One* patiently to bear the implacable hatred of *sinners* against himself [*Is* 53:7]. 'The constant consideration of Christ in his sufferings is the best means to keep

up faith unto its due exercise in all times of trial' (John Owen).
[1 *Pet* 2:21–24]

*V*4: **Ye have not yet resisted unto blood, striving against sin:**

Unlike 'the captain of their salvation' the Hebrews have not as yet suffered death in striving against sin, though they have 'endured a great conflict of sufferings' because of their confession of faith in him [10:32–34]. The particular sin of unbelief to which these unexpected hardships had exposed them is here personified as a formidable foe who must be resisted even at the cost of life itself. 'This sin would win if in fear of blood the readers would relinquish their faith; it would be vanquished if the readers, unafraid of a bloody death, held fast to their faith' (Lenski).

*V*5: **and ye have forgotten the exhortation which reasoneth with you as with sons,**
> **My son, regard not lightly the chastening of the Lord,**
> **Nor faint when thou art reproved of him;**

*V*6: **For whom the Lord loveth he chasteneth,**
> **And scourgeth every son whom he receiveth.**

The readers were repining under the opposition they encountered because they had forgotten the Scripture that addresses them as children who must receive with meekness the chastening of their heavenly Father [*Prov* 3:11, 12; cf *Job* 5:17; *Ps* 94:12; *Rev* 3:19]. Although the hard-hearted man steels himself against feeling the stroke, and the faint-hearted man reels under it, the child of God is neither to despise correction nor to despair when he is reproved; otherwise he will fail to profit from the experience.

For whom the Lord loveth he chasteneth, God punishes his enemies; he chastens his children. The one is the judicial infliction of his wrath; the other is the proof of his parental love. 'The same hand – but not the same character – gives the stroke, to the godly and the ungodly. The scourge of the Judge is widely different from the rod of the Father' (Charles Bridges, *Commentary on Proverbs*, p. 31 n.). Moreover, this fatherly discipline pertains only to the present life. 'There is no chastisement in heaven, nor in hell. Not in heaven, because there is no sin; not in hell, because there is no amendment. Chastisement is a companion of them that *are in the way*, and of them only' (John Owen).

*V*7: **It is for chastening that ye endure; God dealeth with you as with sons; for what son is there whom his father chasteneth not?**

If they would endure rightly, they must endure intelligently (Moffatt). They must recognize that the reason for such chastening is found in God's fatherly relation to them, for what son is there whom his father does not correct? 'Corrections are pledges of our adoption and badges of our sonship. One Son God hath without sin, but none without sorrow. As God corrects none but his own, so all that are his shall be sure to have it; and they shall take it for a favour too, 1 Cor 11:32' (Trapp).

*V*8: **But if ye are without chastening, whereof all have been made partakers, then are ye bastards, and not sons.**

These weary Hebrews might well think that they would not suffer if they were really God's sons, but in fact the reverse is the case. For if they did not so suffer, they would not be God's sons! 'Saints, saith God, think not that I hate you, because I thus chide you. He that escapes reprehension may suspect his adoption. God had one Son without corruption, but no son without correction. A gracious soul may look through the darkest cloud, and see a God smiling on him' (Thomas Brooks, *Precious Remedies against Satan's Devices*, pp. 85–86).

[176]

*V*9: **Furthermore, we had the fathers of our flesh to chasten us, and we gave them reverence: shall we not much rather be in subjection unto the Father of spirits, and live?**

'This comparison is made in several parts. The first is that if we give so much reverence to the fathers of whom we are born after the flesh that we submit to their discipline, much more honour is due to God who is our spiritual Father. The second is that the discipline by which fathers bring up their children is only useful for this present life, but God looks further to sanctify us for eternal life. Thirdly, mortal men chastise their children as they think good, but God applies His discipline with the wisest purpose and the highest wisdom so that there is nothing in it that is out of control' (Calvin).

and live? 'We are reminded by this that nothing is more fatal to us than to refuse to give ourselves in obedience to God' (Calvin).

*V*10: **For they indeed for a few days chastened us as seemed good to them; but he for our profit, that we may be partakers of his holiness.**

'The fathers of our flesh' chastened us according to what 'seemed good to them', but God with unerring wisdom designs it for our spiritual good. 'What the Author means to bring out by saying that the chastisement of earthly parents is for a few days, is the brevity and comparative unimportance of our connection with our natural parents; their chastisement is for a short time as the duration of our relation to them is short, and indeed their chastisement, if wise, has in view to make us able to be independent of them; God's chastening has another view, to make us partakers of His holiness, to unite us to Him in character and likeness more and more. It is not the duration of the chastisement that is the point of the passage; it is the duration of our relation in each case to him who chastens' (A. B. Davidson).

*V*11: **All chastening seemeth for the present to be not joyous but grievous; yet afterward it yieldeth peaceable fruit unto them that have been exercised thereby, even the fruit of righteousness.**

Certainly no chastening is regarded as an enjoyable experience at the time, but rather grievous. But it later yields peaceable fruit to those who have been exercised by it, even (the fruit of) 'righteousness,' the word being placed last in the sentence for emphasis. The stoical endurance of that which was intended to be *felt* can never produce such fruit! [*Is* 9:8–12] For it is only when we are 'exercised' by this discipline that a harvest of righteousness is reaped in our lives. And it is indeed 'peaceable fruit' because the victory of faith brings peace in God and peace of conscience.

*V*12: **Wherefore lift up the hands that hang down, and the palsied knees;**
*V*13: **and make straight paths for your feet, that that which is lame be not turned out of the way, but rather be healed.**

The practical application of this teaching is couched in language which is evidently taken from *Is* 35:3 and *Prov* 4:26. In *v* 12 the bracing of the body stands for the spiritual resolution with which Christians are to meet adversity. Instead of wilting under chastisement, they are to lift up the listless hands and strengthen the paralysed knees.

and make straight paths for your feet, that that which is lame be not put out of joint but rather be healed. (ASV margin) No advance in the Christian way is possible while the community halts between two opinions, for they cannot follow the straight path of grace until they make a final break with Judaism [1 *Kings* 18:21]. 'Inconsistency and vacillation in the general body of the church would create a way so difficult for the lame, that their lameness would become dislocation, and they would perish from the way; on the other hand, the habit of going in a plain path would restore them to soundness' (A. B. Davidson).

*V*14: **Follow after peace with all men, and the sanctification without which no man shall see the Lord:**

The following verses [*vv* 14–17] set forth the indispensable conditions for receiving the promised blessings of the gospel.

Peace continue to pursue with all, (Lenski). If this were one of a series of general admonitions, the reference would be to 'all men' [cf *Rom* 12:18], but in the present context the thought centres on 'the crippled souls' in their company and so the parallel is *Rom* 14:19: 'peace with all the members of the church so that no dissension may afford anyone cause for turning from Christ' (Lenski).

and the sanctification without which no man shall see the Lord: 'Sanctification' is well described by Westcott as 'the preparation for the presence of God'. It is 'the bringing of the consecrated person into harmony of life and character with the consecration' (Vaughan). As the Hebrew believers had been separated unto God by their confession of faith in Christ, so they are to live the life that befits those who are so separated [cf *Rom* 6:19, 22].

*V*15: **looking carefully lest there be any man that falleth short of the grace of God; lest any root of bitterness springing up trouble you, and thereby the many be defiled;**

looking carefully whether there be any man that falleth back from the grace of God, (ASV margin) It would be foolish to infer from this that the saints of God can fall from grace and be lost, because the author has in view only the 'phenomenal aspect of religion' (Vos). He is making the simple point that anyone who abandons his profession of Christ in favour of a return to Judaism is left behind in the wilderness of unbelief, and it is to guard against this danger that he exhorts them all to be overseers of one another [3:12f].

lest any root of bitterness springing up trouble you, and thereby the many be defiled; If anyone among them thus falls back from gospel grace, it is not merely a loss for himself, it is also a danger for many others. Such a man would be like the springing up of a bitter root which spreads its defilement to the whole congregation, so making it unfit to worship God [*Deut* 29:18; *Josh* 7:25]. 'Himself bitter against Christ, he embitters others against Christ, poisons them, if you will' (Lenski). [cf *Gal* 5:9]

*V*16: **lest there be any fornicator, or profane person, as Esau, who for one mess of meat sold his own birthright.**

By recalling Esau's irrevocable act of folly, the author now warns the waverers that spiritual blessings when once renounced cannot be regained [*vv* 16, 17]. The reference is not to sexual immorality, which is dealt with later in the Epistle [13:4], but to the peril of religious infidelity. The 'fornication' that he has in mind is illustrated by the profane choice of Esau, who forfeited the blessing of God in favour of a paltry secular benefit. Thus the word 'fornicator' is 'used here in the Biblical sense of idolater' (R. V. G. Tasker).

who for one mess of meat sold his own birthright. As the first-born, Esau possessed spiritual privileges which were distinctively his own, until he rashly bartered them away for a miserable morsel of meat – such a 'cheap meal', says Calvin, as that 'by which Satan habitually lures the reprobate' [*Gen* 25:29–34].

[180]

V17: For ye know that even when he afterward desired to inherit the blessing, he was rejected; for he found no place for a change of mind in his father, though he sought it diligently with tears.

Now the warning is driven home. For the Hebrews know that though Esau afterward desired to have the blessing he had despised, he found it impossible to reverse the consequences of his sinful choice. In fact his profane irreverence was further manifested in the desire to occupy the place he had so light-heartedly abandoned. Having sold his birthright as something of no value, he nevertheless desired *to inherit* the blessing which belonged to it! 'He asserted the prerogative of birth, a gift of God, when he had himself recklessly surrendered it' (Westcott).

(for he found no place of repentance), (ASV margin) It is going against the natural construction of the words to refer this repentance to a change of mind on the part of Isaac (as in the ASV text). It was Esau who sought but could not find a place of 'repentance'. The word as used here means more than a mere change of mind; it refers to 'a change of mind undoing the effects of a former state of mind' (A. B. Davidson). The message for the readers is loud and clear: It is 'impossible again to renew to repentance' those who wilfully renounce their spiritual birthright, for after the gospel has been rejected there is no place for a change of mind which will secure them the final blessing [6:6, 10:26].

though he sought it diligently with tears. 'It' being the blessing he now so belatedly desired. 'He might have had it formerly without tears; afterwards, though weeping, he was rejected' (Bengel). [*Gen* 27:34f]

V18: For ye are not come unto a mount that might be touched, and that burned with fire, and unto blackness, and darkness, and tempest,

*V*19: **and the sound of a trumpet, and the voice of words; which voice they that heard entreated that no word more should be spoken unto them;**

The issue facing the Hebrews is now crystallized in one magnificent sentence [*vv* 18-24]. As the superiority of the new covenant infinitely transcends that of the old economy which it has superseded, so those who despise the grace so fully exhibited in it will be visited by sanctions even more severe than those which attended the giving of the law [2:2-4]. The welcome absence of the awesome sensible phenomena which characterized the Sinaitic revelation must not lead them to doubt the ultimate reality of that supersensible world to which they have been brought by the gospel. For the very same voice which spoke to the people from a material mountain now addresses them from heaven itself! Well might the author earnestly urge them to 'See that ye refuse not him that speaketh' [*v* 25]. [Cf *Exod* 19:16-19; 20:18-21; *Deut* 4:11f]

which voice they that heard entreated that no word more should be spoken unto them; As the people heard the direct speech of God from out of the fire and darkness which surrounded the mount they were stricken with terror, for 'the speaking of the law doth immediately discover the invincible necessity of a mediator between God and sinners' (John Owen). [*Exod* 20:19; *Deut* 5:25]

*V*20: **for they could not endure that which was enjoined, If even a beast touch the mountain, it shall be stoned;** *V*21: **and so fearful was the appearance, that Moses said, I exceedingly fear and quake:**

Moreover, the fact that the people could not bear the rigour of the command to slay by stoning any trespassing beast clearly showed that this approach to God was at the same time a fearful shrinking back. Although the words attributed to Moses are not an exact quotation from the Old Testament, there is no need to doubt that they accurately represent his state of mind on that occasion. For if only the *remembrance* of the sight led him to express himself in similar terms [*Deut* 9:19], he must have been even more terrified by the reality itself [cf *Exod* 19:10ff].

'The effect of this terror extended itself unto the meanest of beasts, and unto the best of men,' and, argues John Owen, if the 'mediator himself of the old covenant was not able to sustain the dread and terror of the law: how desperate then are their hopes who would yet be saved by Moses!' (i.e. by their obedience to the law, cf *Rom* 10:1–5).

*V*22: **but ye are come unto mount Zion, and unto the city of the living God, the heavenly Jerusalem, and to innumerable hosts of angels,**
*V*23: **to the general assembly and church of the firstborn who are enrolled in heaven, and to God the Judge of all, and to the spirits of just men made perfect,**
*V*24: **and to Jesus the mediator of a new covenant, and to the blood of sprinkling that speaketh better than that of Abel.**

but ye are come unto mount Zion, and unto the city of the living God, the heavenly Jerusalem, Mount Zion is here spiritualized to suggest an image of that heavenly realm to which the Hebrews have already been brought by grace. Thus in leaving Mount Sinai for Mount Zion they have exchanged the sensuous for the spiritual; the place of temporal manifestation for the eternal abode of the righteous; and the dread sense of separation from God for the gracious privilege of unbroken communion with God through Jesus Christ. 'As Jerusalem was distinguished into two cities, the superior and the inferior; so is the Church into triumphant and militant; yet both make up but one city of the living God' (Trapp).

and to innumerable angels in festal gathering, (RSV) 'Sinai, too, had its angels, but they did not appear in festal assembly, see *Acts* 7:53 and *Gal* 3:19. The word "myriads" or ten thousands is repeatedly used with reference to angels [*Dan* 7:10; *Jude* 14; *Rev* 5:11]. Since Christ has entered heaven after his work of redemption, the whole angel world rings with festal panegyrics [*Rev* 5:1–12]' (Lenski).

and to the assembly of the first-born who are enrolled in heaven, (RSV) Those who still tread the pilgrim path on earth may rejoice in the knowledge that their names are already written in heaven, and that before long they will join that vast company which forms the church triumphant [*Luke* 10:20; *Rev* 21:27]. 'All the people of Christ are the "first-born" children of God, through their union with Him who is The First-born *par excellence*; their birthright is not to be bartered away, as was Esau's' (F. F. Bruce).

and to a judge who is God of all, (RSV) This reminder that they have already come before a judge who is the God of all creation serves a dual purpose. For God is both the *discerner* of the true among the professing (a note of warning), and 'the *avenger* of the true Church, now under persecution and temptation (a note of comfort)' (Vaughan). [10:27, 30, 31; *Luke* 18:7, 8]

and to the spirits of just men made perfect, 'The souls of the just when separated from their bodies, do not wander up and down in this world, nor hover about the sepulchres where their bodies lie; nor are they detained in any purgatory, in order to their more perfect purification; nor do they fall asleep in a benumbed stupid state: but do forthwith pass into glory, and are immediately with the Lord' (John Flavel, *Works*, Vol. III, p. 38). [*Luke* 23:43]

and to Jesus the mediator of a new covenant, In contrast to the antiquated covenant which it replaced, this 'new' (*neos*) covenant is both recently established and ever fresh and young. Its Mediator is here simply called 'Jesus'–'the *human* name so full of the *saving* character [*Matt* 1:21], so attractive therefore to the struggling and militant church' (Vaughan). 'Believers have not now access unto, or dependence on, a Moses, a mere man, and a servant, declaring God's will, only a sinner himself, trembling in his office, and weary of his clients, and whose ministry is vanishing, as his person dying; but unto God the Son himself incarnate, a Son-mediator, making sons, and bringing them nearer to God, satisfying the law for them and writing it on their hearts; above all sin himself, though a sacrifice for it, who is able to save to the uttermost, for that he ever liveth to intercede for them, *ch* 1:1–3, 3:6, 7:26; *Rev* 1:13' (Poole).

and to the blood of sprinkling that speaketh better than that of Abel. Abel and Jesus were both slain by wicked hands, but whereas Abel's blood cried for vengeance on him by whom it was shed, that of Jesus pleads for the pardon of guilty sinners, and so speaks 'better' than a martyr's blood [*Gen* 4:10; *Luke* 23:34]. It is here called 'the blood of sprinkling' since it cleanses only those to whom it is applied in faith [1 *John* 1:7].

*V*25: **See that ye refuse not him that speaketh. For if they escaped not when they refused him that warned them on earth, much more shall not we escape who turn away from him that warneth from heaven:**

The preceding comparison is enforced by a final appeal not to capitulate to the prompting of unbelief which could stifle the voice which still speaks to them in grace from heaven [2:2f, 10:29]. In the *innocent* request that God should not speak directly to them at Sinai, the author 'sees *prefigured* the *sinful* refusals of the voice of God in the onward history of Israel, and draws a note of warning from them for Christian days' (Vaughan). [cf 3:7ff]

*V*26: **whose voice then shook the earth: but now he hath promised, saying, Yet once more will I make to tremble not the earth only, but also the heaven.**
*V*27: **And this word, Yet once more, signifieth the removing of those things that are shaken, as of things that have been made, that those things which are not shaken may remain.**

At Sinai God's voice shook the earth, but according to *Haggai* 2:6 there is a day coming when he will shake both heaven and earth. By underlining the words, 'yet once more', he shows us that the second shaking will be final. It will sweep away all things temporal so that the unshakeable eternal realities may remain. The forthcoming consummation thus has a positive purpose: it is the establishment of a new heaven and a new earth which shall become the heritage of the redeemed [2:5; *Rom* 8:19; 2 *Pet* 3:13; *Rev* 21:1–5]. If therefore the Hebrews would not fall short of this eternal inheritance, they must not refuse to hear what God in these last days is speaking to them in his Son.

*V*28: **Wherefore, receiving a kingdom that cannot be shaken, let us have grace, whereby we may offer service well-pleasing to God with reverence and awe:**
*V*29: **for our God is a consuming fire.**

'Let us have grace' is more accurately rendered 'let us be thankful' (Arndt-Gingrich). The grace which has invested them with all the privileges of citizenship in an immovable kingdom must constrain an overwhelming sense of gratitude to God. This will find its natural expression in service that is well-pleasing to him because it proceeds from those whose lives are permeated by 'godly fear and awe' (ASV margin). This reverential fear of God accompanies every genuine experience of his redeeming love, for the nearer we are brought to God by grace, the greater will be our sense of the infinite gulf which separates the creature from the Creator [cf *Is* 6:1f].

for our God is a consuming fire. These words are taken from *Deut* 4:24 which warns Israel that their covenant relationship with God ('*our* God') would not protect them from the devouring fire of divine judgment if they incurred his jealousy by lapsing into the sin of idolatry. An abiding consciousness of the ineffable holiness of God offers the best deterrent against the commission of sin, and therefore every child of grace prays, 'Unite my heart to fear thy name', for he knows that it is impossible to combine a love of sin with a love for God [*Ps* 86:11]. 'Even those who stand highest in the love and favour of God, and have the fullest assurance thereof, and of their interest in Him as their God, ought, notwithstanding, to fear Him as a sin-revenging God and a consuming fire' (Ezekiel Hopkins: Sermon on Heb. 12:28, 29).

CHAPTER THIRTEEN

After various exhortations concerning social and religious duties, there is a final appeal to renounce the vain ritual of a superseded order and to share Christ's reproach by joining him outside the camp of Judaism [vv 1–17]. The author requests the prayers of his readers that he might soon be restored to them, and formally concludes the letter with a majestic benediction and doxology [vv 18–21]. He urges them to heed his word of exhortation, gives news of Timothy's release, sends greetings, and ends with a brief benediction [vv 22–25].

The author's 'word of exhortation' [v 22] is more like a homily than a letter, but in his concluding words he reverts to Paul's familiar pattern of reminding the readers of their obligation to live out what they believe. He begins his 'ethical' appendix with a brief paragraph of crisp precepts which set forth the Christian's social duties [vv 1–6].

V1: **Let love of the brethren continue.**

Whenever this command is 'more honoured in the breach than the observance', Christianity ceases to exist, for God refuses to accept the professed service of those who are without love for the brethren. Hence the need to insist upon the *continuance* of this love! The primary importance of this injunction makes it unnecessary to imagine that it was called forth by any particular situation. It is everywhere insisted upon throughout the New Testament [e.g. *John* 13:34; *Rom* 13:8; 1 *Cor* 13; 1 *Thess* 4:9; 1 *Pet* 1:22; 1 *John* 2:10; 3:11, 23; 4:7, 11, 12, 21]. As Westcott observes: 'The love of the Jew for his fellow Jew, his "brother", was national: the Christian's love for his fellow-Christian is catholic. The tie of the common faith is universal, and in proportion as the ill-will of those without increased, it became necessary to deepen the feeling of affection within'.

V2: **Forget not to show love unto strangers: for thereby some have entertained angels unawares.**

A readiness to welcome travellers and a compassionate concern for those under affliction are two ways in which this brotherly love is to be manifested [*vv* 2, 3]. They must not neglect to offer hospitality to strangers for in so doing 'some have entertained angels unawares', not as though they will receive such supernatural visitors as Abraham once did, but they may well find that some of their guests resemble *angels* (i.e. messengers) in proving to be true *messengers* of God to them [*Gen* 18]. Moffatt points out that there were pressing reasons for the exercise of this kindly virtue in the primitive church, because inns were notorious not only for their extortionate charges but also for their low moral standards. Such accommodation was obviously unsuitable for travelling Christians on both these counts.

V3: **Remember them that are in bonds, as bound with them; them that are ill-treated, as being yourselves also in the body.**

But while strangers seek hospitality [*v* 2], prisoners must be sought out in order to be helped. From the foundation of the church, Christians, in obedience to the Lord's teaching [*Matt* 25:36], and often at great risk to themselves, ministered to the needs of such as suffered imprisonment for the gospel's sake. This help was given in several ways: either by personally visiting them to alleviate their suffering through gifts and sympathy [2 *Tim* 1:16], or by subscribing money to purchase their release, or by praying for them [*Col* 4:3, 18]. The author next bids his readers remember that they also are in the body; for when one member of the Christian community suffers, all the members suffer with it [1 *Cor* 12:26]. 'This is the ideal which each believer must strive to realize' (Westcott).

*V*4: **Let marriage be had in honour among all, and let the bed be undefiled: for fornicators and adulterers God will judge.**

After mention of the body, the sanctity of the marriage bond is next enforced. This is not a statement defending marriage against a false asceticism as the AV wrongly suggests, but a serious warning not to indulge in any sexual relationship outside that honourable estate. Since sin entered the world human society always has been permissive, but Christians have been rescued from this degradation by the amazing grace of God [1 *Cor* 6:9–11]. Fornicators and adulterers generally escape human condemnation, but *God* (placed last in the sentence for emphasis) will judge those whom man does not punish [10:30]. And then the immoralities which now are so flippantly regarded will be viewed in a very different light!

*V*5: **Be ye free from the love of money; content with such things as ye have: for himself hath said, I will in no wise fail thee, neither will I in any wise forsake thee.**
*V*6: **So that with good courage we say,**

> **The Lord is my helper; I will not fear:**
> **What shall man do unto me?**

Finally, Christians must be free of the *love* of money, which Paul says is the root of all evil [1 *Tim* 6:10]; and be content with what they have, knowing that with God as their satisfying portion they will lack for nothing [*Matt* 6:31–33]. This exhortation is supported by two quotations which confirm that the assurance of God's presence with them should remove all anxious care. As the first of these recalls the words of encouragement given to Joshua when their forefathers were on the verge of entering Canaan [*Josh* 1:5], there is a peculiar fitness in applying it to the crisis which these Jewish Christians were now facing. The second is taken from *Ps* 118:6, and it expresses the response they ought to be able to make to the promise of God's perpetual presence. 'If He has said, I will never leave, WE may well say, What shall MAN do?' (John Brown). [cf *Rom* 8:31f]

*V*7: **Remember them that had the rule over you, men that spake unto you the word of God; and considering the issue of their life, imitate their faith.**

The closing appeal makes it clear that fidelity to Christ demands a final break with Judaism and involves the bearing of his reproach outside the camp [*vv* 7–17]. 'There would be no meaning in exhorting the Hebrews to remember their former teachers unless the exhortation were an indirect way of exhorting them not to swerve from the faith in the form in which those departed teachers had delivered it to them' (A. B. Davidson). A consideration of the end of their pilgrimage provides the grand incentive to imitate their faith. The Hebrews cannot expect to finish their earthly course in the same way unless they abide in the same faith. Although these leaders died in the faith they had so long confessed, there is no need to assume that they also died as martyrs for it, as some have suggested.

*V*8: **Jesus Christ is the same yesterday and to-day, yea and for ever,**

The verse affirms that Jesus Christ is still the same to-day as he was yesterday declared to be by their former teachers [*v* 7], and he will remain the same throughout eternity. This declaration of an unchanging Christ is therefore a summons to an unchangeable faith in him. Hence Trapp remarks, 'This was the sum of their sermons, and is the substance of their and your faith; which therefore you must stick to, standing fast in the street which is called Straight, *Acts* 9:11, and not whirred about with divers and strange doctrines'.

*V*9: **Be not carried away by divers and strange teachings: for it is good that the heart be established by grace; not by meats, wherein they that occupied themselves were not profited.**

Be not carried away by divers and strange teachings: 'He calls the teachings which lead us away from Christ *diverse*, since there is no other simple and pure truth than the knowledge of Christ. He calls them *strange*, since God does not regard as His anything that is outside Christ. By this we are warned how we should proceed if we want to attain due proficiency in Scripture, for anyone who does not take a straight course to Christ is a wanderer' (Calvin).

for it is good that the heart be established by grace; Their hearts cannot be made firm without their determined adherence to the doctrine they had already received, because the gospel is the sole channel through which the saving grace of God is mediated to mankind.

not by meats, wherein they that walked were not profited. (ASV margin) Since the meticulous observance of such distinctions did not profit those who practised them, it would be sheer folly to exchange the principle of grace for the empty ritual of a vanished order. As the writer goes on to say 'we have an altar', the word 'meats' almost certainly refers to the priestly privilege of partaking in those sacred meals which were provided by meat which had been first offered in sacrifice. The main point to be grasped is that the difference between 'grace' and 'meats' – between the Christian faith and Judaism – is one of complete antithesis. For the grace of the gospel cannot co-exist with the lifeless performance of an external religious code, which is here summed up in the pregnant term 'meats' [cf 9:10]. 'The Apostle refers to "teachings", not to practices; it is not implied that the Hebrews were in a locality where the practices were carried on, they were being carried aside by the doctrines' (A. B. Davidson).

V10: **We have an altar, whereof they have no right to eat that serve the tabernacle.**

Although Christians do not have a visible altar on which many kinds of sacrifices are offered, this does not mean that they are without an altar of their own. This 'altar' is Christ's once-for-all sacrifice which fulfilled what was foreshadowed on the Day of Atonement. On that occasion no part of the offering was reserved for the priests, for after the high priest had presented the blood within the sanctuary, the bodies of the beasts were burned outside the camp [*Lev* 16:27]. Accordingly those who continue to 'serve the tabernacle' thereby debar themselves from any part in the offering of Christ. The benefits which Christ purchased for his people by his death cannot be enjoyed by those who remain inside the camp which crucified the Lord of glory! The observations of John Owen on this verse have lost none of their force over the years, and they are as pertinent today as when they were first written.

'*Obs. I.* That the Lord Christ, in the one sacrifice of himself, is the only altar of the church of the new testament.

Obs. II. That this altar is every way sufficient in itself for the end of an altar, namely, the sanctification of the people; as *v* 12.

Obs. III. The erection of any other altar in the church or, the introduction of any other sacrifice requiring a material altar, is derogatory to the sacrifice of Christ, and exclusive of him from being our altar'.

V11: **For the bodies of those beasts whose blood is brought into the holy place by the high priest as an offering for sin, are burned without the camp.**
V12: **Wherefore Jesus also, that he might sanctify the people through his own blood, suffered without the gate.**

It was because all the sins of the congregation were laid upon the bodies of these beasts that they were devoted to destruction outside the camp. In the same way Christ the sinless One became an outcast when the sins of his people were laid to his account, and he suffered outside the gate in order to exhaust the curse he bore for them [*Gal* 3:13]. It was this vicarious bearing of the curse of sin which effected the sanctification of those he represented. Moreover, this suffering not only served to separate a people unto himself, it also finally severed his connection with an apostate nation. 'When the Lord Jesus carried all the sins of his own people in his own body unto the tree, he left the city, as a type of all unbelievers, under the wrath and curse of God' (John Owen).

V13: **Let us therefore go forth unto him without the camp, bearing his reproach.**
V14: **For we have not here an abiding city, but we seek after the city which is to come.**

The climax of the Epistle is reached in this moving appeal. No place remains for the Hebrews within the city which had rejected and crucified their Lord (a statement which would have little point if Jerusalem had already been destroyed). They must abandon the rites and ceremonies of Judaism from which the glory had departed, in order to join Christ outside the camp, for it is impossible to evade bearing his reproach without also losing his presence [11:26; *Luke* 9:23; *Phil*

3:4-10]. Furthermore, any reluctance to renounce the protection of those religious privileges which were centred upon an earthly city would be dispelled by remembering that their real security lay in remaining faithful to their heavenly calling. 'The main business of believers in this world is diligently to seek after the city of God, or the attainment of eternal rest with him; and this is the character whereby they may be known' (John Owen). [11:10, 13–16; *Phil* 3:20]

*V*15: **Through him then let us offer up a sacrifice of praise to God continually, that is, the fruit of lips which make confession to his name.**

John Owen notes that the next three verses give a summary of Christian duty under three heads: *Spiritual*, with respect to God, *v* 15; *Moral*, with respect to men, *v* 16; and *Ecclesiastical*, with respect to Christian leaders, *v* 17.

Through him then 'Through him' is the same as *through him alone*. 'There is a profane opinion and practice in the papal church about offering our sacrifices of prayer and praise to God by others; as by saints and angels, especially the blessed Virgin. But are they our altar? Did they sanctify us by their blood? Did they suffer for us without the gate? Are they the high priests of the church? Have they made us priests unto God; or prepared a new and living way for our entrance unto the throne of grace? It is on account of these things that we are said to offer our sacrifice by Christ; and it is the highest blasphemy to assign them unto any other'. It therefore follows that, 'Whatever we tender unto God, and not by Christ, it hath no other acceptance with him than the sacrifice of Cain' (John Owen).

let us offer up a sacrifice of praise to God continually, The sacrifices which believers now offer are not carnal but spiritual. They are the sacrifices of praise and thanksgiving, of beneficence and almsgiving [*v* 16]. Clearly, as defined

[195]

here and elsewhere in the New Testament, true worship is essentially inward and ethical [cf *Rom* 12:1, 2; *James* 1:27].

that is, the fruit of lips which make confession to his name. In the passage here quoted the prophet makes a figurative use of sacrificial language in order vividly to express the reality of Israel's repentance [cf *Ps* 50:12-15, 51:15-17]. 'Covering God's altar with the calves of our lips, Hos. 14.3. This shall please the Lord better than an ox or bullock that hath horns and hoofs; *Ps* 69:31' (Trapp).

*V*16: **But to do good and to communicate forget not: for with such sacrifices God is well pleased.**

The sincerity of their love for God will be shown by a practical concern for the needs of others [1 *John* 3:17]. As they have been careful to do this very thing in the past, so they are to maintain the same ministry in the future [6:10]. This fellowship is sacrificial because it involves the Christian in sharing his temporal blessings with those in need, and with such service God is well pleased. Moreover, he who has freely received, will freely give, for an experience of grace is always reflected in a life of gratitude [*Matt* 25:35-40; *Rom* 12:13; *Gal* 6:6; *Phil* 4:18].

*V*17: **Obey them that have the rule over you, and submit to them: for they watch in behalf of your souls, as they that shall give account; that they may do this with joy, and not with grief: for this were unprofitable for you.**

The author previously referred to the fidelity of their former leaders in the faith; now he urges them to obey their present guides [*vv* 7, 17]. 'It is their duty so to *obey* whilst they (the rulers) teach the things which the Lord Christ hath appointed them to teach; for unto them is their commission limited, *Matt* 28:20: and to *submit unto their rule* whilst it is exercised in the name of Christ, according to his institution, and by the rule of the word, and not otherwise. When they depart from these, there is neither obedience nor submission due unto them' (John Owen).

for they watch in behalf of your souls, as they that shall give account; that they may do this with joy, and not with grief: Like faithful shepherds, they watch in the interest of your souls, and they do this under the constant pressure of knowing that one day they must render to the Chief Shepherd an account of the care they have taken of his sheep. For if you are unwilling to obey their teaching, they will not be able to render a joyful account of their oversight on the great day of reckoning [*v* 20; *Ezek* 33:7–9; *Phil* 2:16]. **for this were unprofitable for you.** An impressive understatement! 'While *they* groan, *you* would do worse than groan. All the advantage of having faithful leaders and watchmen would not only be lost but would turn into the opposite. It is bad when no one rings the alarm and warns, it is a thousand times worse for you and for me when we are deaf to a true warning' (Lenski). [2 *Thess* 1:7–9]

*V*18: **Pray for us: for we are persuaded that we have a good conscience, desiring to live honourably in all things.**
*V*19: **And I exhort you the more exceedingly to do this, that I may be restored to you the sooner.**

In referring to himself for the first time, the author requests the prayers of his readers. 'The allusion to his purity of conduct, and strong assertion of his consciousness of it, in regard to them and all things, when he is petitioning for their prayers, implies that some suspicions may have attached to him in the minds of some of them. These suspicions would naturally refer to his great freedom in regard to Jewish practices' (A. B. Davidson). Although he is not detained in prison [*v* 23], it seems that he is engaged on some mission which hinders his return, but he hopes that he may be soon 'restored' to them. Events would prove whether it was in fact God's will that he should return to them, yet as John Owen wisely observes, prayer is not to be ruled by the secret purposes of God. 'According unto our present apprehensions of duty, we may lawfully have earnest desires after, and pray for such things as shall not come to pass'.

*V*20: **Now the God of peace, who brought again from the dead the great shepherd of the sheep with the blood of an eternal covenant, even our Lord Jesus,**
*V*21: **make you perfect in every good thing to do his will, working in us that which is well-pleasing in his sight, through Jesus Christ; to whom be the glory for ever and ever. Amen.**

Having requested prayer for himself, the author concludes with a marvellously comprehensive prayer for his readers which recapitulates the message of the entire Epistle.

Now the God of peace, who brought again from the dead the great shepherd of the sheep It is in the raising up from the dead of 'our Lord Jesus' that God is known as the 'God of peace', because the resurrection is the proof of our reconciliation. 'Christ, as the great shepherd of the sheep, was brought into the state of death by the sentence of the law; and was thence led, recovered, and restored, by the God of peace . . . Had not the will of God been satisfied, atonement made for sin, the church sanctified, the law accomplished, and the threatenings satisfied, Christ could not have been brought again from the dead . . . The death of Christ, if he had not risen, would not have completed our redemption, we should have been "yet in our sins"; for evidence would have been given that atonement was not made. The bare resurrection of Christ, or the bringing him from the dead, would not have saved us; for so any other man may be raised by the power of God. But the bringing again of Christ from the dead, "through the blood of the everlasting covenant", is that which gives assurance of the complete redemption and salvation of the church' (John Owen). So though Israel had been led by other shepherds in former days, the Hebrews must recognize that it is only by heeding the voice of this 'great shepherd' that they can enjoy God's peace, for he alone ever lives to guide, guard, and rule over the *one* flock of God [*John* 10:1–28; 1 *Pet* 2:25, 5:4].

in the blood of an eternal covenant, (ASV margin) 'In the blood' means that Christ was raised in virtue of his own sacrificial blood-shedding which had abolished the old covenant and established an eternal covenant, so that now 'there is no more offering for sin' [10:18]. If then the resurrection 'is the *result* of the Saviour's sacrifice offered in blood, it is impossible that the Ascension of the Saviour can be *in order* to the offering of that blood of sacrifice in heaven' (N. Dimock, *The Sacerdotium of Christ*, p. 113).

even our Lord Jesus, Since this is the Epistle's only reference to Christ's resurrection, it is significant that the author who has dwelt so lovingly upon the human name 'Jesus' should here add the title 'Lord', thus pointing to the universal dominion with which he was then invested. The appeal of the confessional 'our' should not be overlooked.

make you perfect in every good work to do his will, (AV) Although by nature we are completely unfit to perform any good work, for we have neither the inclination nor the capacity to do God's will, the grace that bestows an interest in 'the blood of the everlasting covenant' imparts the capacity to do works which God accounts 'good' because they are the fruit of our union with Christ ('*through* Jesus Christ'). [*Eph* 2:10]

working in us that which is well-pleasing in his sight,

Nothing but an experience of grace will supply us with the key which enables us to understand the Pauline paradox: 'Whatever good we *do*, God *does* in us [*Phil* 2:13]' (Fausset).

through Jesus Christ, to whom be the glory for ever and ever. Amen. 'The doxology may be to the God of peace to whom the prayer is addressed, more probably it is to Jesus Christ, last-named and the great figure who has been before the mind throughout the Epistle' (Marcus Dods).

*V*22: **But I exhort you, brethren, bear with the word of exhortation: for I have written unto you in few words.**

What follows his prayer is in the nature of a postscript. First he urges them as 'brethren' to 'bear with the word of exhortation' even though it should cut across their most cherished prejudices. 'Sharp though it be, and to the flesh tiresome, yet suffer it. Better it is that the vine should bleed than die. But many are like the nettle, touch it never so gently, it will sting you' (Trapp). In view of the critical decision facing them [*v* 13], he says that he has written briefly. For though the letter is long by New Testament standards, it could be read aloud to the congregation in less than an hour.

*V*23: **Know ye that our brother Timothy hath been set at liberty; with whom, if he come shortly, I will see you.**

Next he informs them of the release of Timothy with whom he hopes to visit them, provided Timothy arrives before he is obliged to start his journey. 'All that we can infer from this reference to an imprisonment of Timothy of which we have no other information is that probably the readers and certainly "the writer stood in some relationship to the Pauline world-mission circle"' (F. F. Bruce).

*V*24: **Salute all them that have the rule over you, and all the saints. They of Italy salute you.**

V25: **Grace be with you all. Amen.**

The usual Christian greetings and the benediction bring the Epistle to a close. If 'they of Italy' refers to those resident in Italy, then the writer is in Italy himself. But it is more likely that this refers to a group living outside Italy, and in that case, the writer, who is also abroad, is addressing a community whose most probable location is Rome. The benediction is identical to that found in Titus. And it is this word 'grace' which sums up all the blessings of that new and better covenant of which Jesus Christ is the sole Mediator.

Soli Deo Gloria

BIBLIOGRAPHY AND ACKNOWLEDGMENTS

The author expresses his grateful thanks to the following authors and publishers who have kindly given permission to reproduce quotations from their copyright works.

Allis, O. T., *Prophecy and the Church* (Presbyterian & Reformed, 1954)

Berkouwer, G. C., *Faith and Perseverance* (Eerdmans, 1958)

Berkouwer, G. C., *The Person of Christ* (Eerdmans, 1954)

Brown, Colin (Editor), *The New International Dictionary of New Testament Theology, Volume 1* (Paternoster Press, 1975)

Bruce, F. F., *The Epistle to the Hebrews* (NLC) (Marshall, Morgan & Scott, 1964)

Calvin, John, *The Epistle to the Hebrews* (translated by William B. Johnston) (Oliver & Boyd, 1963)

Cullmann, Oscar, *The Christology of the New Testament* (SCM, 1963)

Denney, James, *The Death of Christ* (Tyndale, 1964)

Hewitt, Thomas, *Hebrews – Introduction and Commentary* (TNTC) (Tyndale, 1960)

Kidner, Derek, *Psalms 1–72 – Introduction and Commentary* (TOTC) (Tyndale, 1973)

Kittel, G. and Friedrich, G., *Theological Dictionary of the New Testament* (translated by Geoffrey W. Bromiley; Index by Ronald E. Pitkin) (Vols. 1–10) (Eerdmans, 1964–76)

Lenski, R. C. H., *The Interpretation of the Epistle to the Hebrews* (Augsburg, 1961)

McKelvey, R. J., *The New Temple* (OUP, 1969)

Morris, Leon, *The Apostolic Preaching of the Cross* (Tyndale Press, 1965)

Murray, John, *Collected Writings: 1. The Claims of Truth* (Banner of Truth, 1976)

Murray, John, *Collected Writings: 2. Systematic Theology* (Banner of Truth, 1977)

Murray, John, *The Covenant of Grace* (Tyndale, 1956)

Murray, John, *Redemption Accomplished and Applied* (Banner of Truth, 1961)

Neil, William, *The Epistle to the Hebrews* (Torch) (SCM, 1955)

Robertson, A. T., *Word Pictures of the New Testament, Vol. V* (Broadman, 1932)

Stibbs, A. M., *The Finished Work of Christ* (Tyndale, 1955)

Stibbs, A. M., *The Meaning of the Word 'Blood' in Scripture* (Tyndale, 1958)

Stibbs, A. M., *Commentary on Hebrews* (NBC – Revised) (IVP, 1970)

Tasker, R. V. G., *The Gospel in the Epistle to the Hebrews* (Tyndale, 1956)

Vine, W. E., *Expository Dictionary of New Testament Words* (Oliphants, 1958)

Vos, Geerhardus, *Biblical Theology* (Banner of Truth, 1975)

Vos, Geerhardus, *The Self-Disclosure of Jesus* (Eerdmans, 1954)

Vos, Geerhardus, *The Teaching of the Epistle to the Hebrews* (Eerdmans, 1956)

Wyngaarden, Martin J., *The Future of the Kingdom in Prophecy and Fulfilment* (Baker, 1955)

In addition to these, the following books were consulted:

Arndt, W. F. and Gingrich, F. W., *A Greek-English Lexicon of the New Testament* (University of Chicago Press, 1957)

Bengel, J. A., *New Testament Word Studies* (Kregel, 1971)

Berkhof, L., *Systematic Theology* (Banner of Truth, 1959)

Boettner, Loraine, *Roman Catholicism* (Banner of Truth, 1966)

Bridges, Charles, *Commentary on Proverbs* (Banner of Truth, 1968)

Brown, John, *The Epistle to the Hebrews* (Banner of Truth, 1972)

Burroughs, Jeremiah, *The Rare Jewel of Christian Contentment* (Banner of Truth, 1964)

Cunningham, William, *Historical Theology* (Banner of Truth, 1960)

Davidson, A. B., *Hebrews* (HBC) (T & T Clark, 1959)

BIBLIOGRAPHY

Delitzsch, Franz, *Commentary on the Epistle to the Hebrews* (T & T Clark, 1880)

Dimock, Nathaniel, *Our One Priest on High* (Longmans, Green, 1910)

Dimock, Nathaniel, *The Sacerdotium of Christ* (Longmans, Green, 1910)

Dods, Marcus, *The Epistle to the Hebrews* (EGT) (Eerdmans, 1974)

Fausset, A. R., *Hebrews* (JFB) (Collins, 1874)

Flavel, John, *Works, Vols. I & III* (Banner of Truth, 1968)

Guthrie, Donald, *New Testament Introduction* (Tyndale Press, 1970)

Henry, Matthew, *Commentary on the Holy Bible* (various editions)

Hodge, A. A., *The Atonement* (Evangelical Press, 1974)

Hodge, Charles, *Commentary on I Corinthians* (Banner of Truth, 1958)

Hughes, Philip E., *Commentary on the Epistle to the Hebrews* (Eerdmans, 1977)

Leupold, H. C., *Exposition of the Psalms* (Baker, 1961)

Lightfoot, J. B., *Commentary on Philippians* (Zondervan, 1968)

Lightfoot, J. B., *Commentary on Colossians and Philemon* (Zondervan, 1961)

Luther, Martin, *Lectures on Hebrews* (*Works, Vol. 29*) (Concordia, 1968)

Machen, J. G., *The Christian View of Man* (Banner of Truth, 1965)

Manson, William, *The Epistle to the Hebrews* (Hodder & Stoughton, 1966)

Moffatt, James, *The Epistle to the Hebrews* (ICC) (T & T Clark, 1924)

Moule, H. C. G., *Outlines of Christian Doctrine* (Hodder & Stoughton, 1894)

Murray, John, *The Epistle to the Romans* (NLC) (Eerdmans, 1960)

Nairne, A., *The Epistle to the Hebrews* (CGT) CUP, 1922)

North, Brownlow, *The Rich Man and Lazarus* (Banner of Truth, 1960)

Owen, John, *An Exposition of Hebrews* (Sovereign Grace Publishers, 1960)

Owen, John, *Works, Vol VII* (Banner of Truth, 1965)

Palmer, Samuel, *The Nonconformist's Catechism* (*Sermons of the Great Ejection*) (Banner of Truth, 1962)

Pink, Arthur W., *An Exposition of Hebrews* (Baker, 1954)

Pink, Arthur W., *The Holy Spirit* (Baker, 1970)

Poole, Matthew, *Commentary on the Holy Bible, Vol. III* (Banner of Truth, 1963)

Rendall, Frederic, *The Epistle to the Hebrews* (Macmillan, 1888)

Reymond, Robert L., *Introductory Studies in Contemporary Theology* (Presbyterian & Reformed, 1968)

Skilton, John (Editor), *The New Testament Student at Work, Vol. 2* (Presbyterian & Reformed, 1975)

Smeaton, George, *The Apostles' Doctrine of the Atonement* (Zondervan, 1957)

Souter, Alexander, *A Pocket Lexicon of the Greek New Testament* (OUP, 1956)

Swete, H. B., *The Ascended Christ* (Macmillan, 1922)

Trapp, John, *Commentary on the New Testament* (Sovereign Grace Book Club, 1958)

Trench, R. C., *Synonyms of the New Testament* (James Clarke, 1961)

Vaughan, C. J., *The Epistle to the Hebrews* (Macmillan, 1890)

Venning, Ralph, *The Plague of Plagues* (Banner of Truth, 1965)

Vincent, Marvin R., *Word Studies in the New Testament* (MacDonald, n.d.)

Warfield, B. B., *The Inspiration and Authority of the Bible* (Marshall, Morgan & Scott, 1959)

Warfield, B. B., *Counterfeit Miracles* (Banner of Truth, 1972)

Westcott, B. F., *The Epistle to the Hebrews* (Eerdmans, 1974)

Wuest, Kenneth S., *Hebrews in the Greek New Testament* (Eerdmans, 1947)